DANCING WITH BIG DATA:
Conversations with the Experts

BRYAN WEMPEN

INHER TANCE
PRESS

INHER TANCE
PRESS

Published by Inheritance Press LLC
Lake Mary, Florida 32746
www.inheritancepress.com

Bio photo by Steph Grant
Jacket design by Tom Morse-Brown

Library of Congress Control Number: 2015943633

ISBN: 978-0-9823859-7-5

Printed in the United States of America

Thank you Michella for the coffee conversations.

A special thanks to my guests on the Thug Metrics Show who shared their time and insight about Big Data, thank you:

William Tincup, Michael Harms, Randy Roberts, Matt Gough, Jessica Miller-Merrell, Matt Charney, Steve Burton, Don MacPherson, Dr. Brent Bannon, Naomi Bloom, Ivan Casanova, David Bernstein, Jason Lauritsen, Damon Cortesi and Dr. Charles Handler.

Contents

Foreword

THERE'S A THEORY IN LEAN THAT says to really understand some-thing, there are two critical components.

First is the approach with a beginner's mind. Forget what you know. As Yoda told us, "You must unlearn what you have learned." And what's good for a Jedi is indeed good for us. Forgetting what we know and discarding preconceived notions allows us to drape ourselves in humil-ity, approach the altar of learning on hands and knees, and ask basic questions that would shame the less enlightened.

The second component is called Gemba. It is the Japanese word for "where work is done." The idea is that the person who knows a job best is the one who performs it. If you want to understand it, you go and talk to that person. There's no better source of information.

What you are about to read (assuming you started on this page, that is) is the result of combining these two powerful ideas and applying them to the topic at hand. I've worked enough with Bryan to know that he's both bright and curious, a dangerous combination. But by putting aside preconceptions about data, seeking out leaders in the field, and asking questions that run the gamut from entry level to quantum mechanics, he's put together a great package of information. Whether you are new to the topic or have been working with Big Data for years, there is sure to be something new, something different, and something inspiring in the coming pages.

You're invited, then, to take the same approach. Forget what you think you know. Unlearn. Be curious. Read the book. Then read it again. I'm confident you'll find enough great ideas to bring you back for more.

—Dwane Lay, SPHR, VP of Customer
Experience at Dovetail Software

Introduction

ONE MORNING I WOKE UP, GRABBED some coffee and fired up my MacBook Pro, then searched the term "big data" on Google. Not shockingly, it returned a billion search results. I started wondering, how does anyone in HR know where to start thinking about big data? I've spent a considerable amount of time thinking about this question. As I start to discover the ins and outs of understanding big data, hopefully these conversations will help HR practitioners get to know some basics. Maybe at the very least you have a good set of questions to go find your own experts to visit with about big data.

It's very obvious that HR has been tracking and measuring the basic people data for many years. Even the smallest HR departments and organizations are measuring turnover, as well as breaking it down into what type of turnover. According to the latest Quantum Workplace's Best Places to Work research, a large percentage of companies of all sizes are measuring engagement and productivity of their workforce. However, my research revealed that it's the amount and complexity of data and how you analyze the data that moves us from measurement firmly into the "big data" category.

The dance with big data is not a new concept for HR, but the recent popularity and movement toward HR participating in big data analysis and more of the data function with organizations is a huge change for the profession. We've been tracking many people metrics for several years, so it now makes sense to mash up this old data with more recent additions of internal and external data for analysis, with hopes of uncovering business intelligence. Dancing with Big Data is a collection of conversations that provide current insights and perspectives from the leading experts from the HR Technology, Human Capital Management, Recruiting, Marketing, Employment Branding, Consumer, Social Analytics and Cyber Security fields on the subject of big data.

Jumping back a few years to 2010, I felt I needed to get myself updated on the current challenges of the HR professional. I was a vendor providing products and services to HR and felt I was out of touch with their day-to-day challenges and responsibilities. I've discovered I learn the best by having discussions with people deep and knowledgeable in their expertise, so my research led me to look for conversations with experts about their successes and failures.

I felt talking with HR professionals doing the job on a regular basis would be a great way for me to discover the trends of what was "keeping HR up at night." To facilitate these regular discussions, I started an Internet radio show called "DriveThruHR." It was a daily 30-minute broadcast during lunch where I interviewed an HR practitioner, structured as a casual conversation. They would share what was top of mind and important to them in HR.

1,000 interviews later and an estimated 1 million downloads of the show, needless to say I'd learned an incredible amount about what the typical HR professional faces in their day-to-day professional lives. These conversations opened my eyes and I found myself thinking about how HR was doing with whole big data movement. After 4+ years of daily interviewing of those in the HR sector, maybe the next chapter for me would be discovering what's up with HR and Big Data?

The big data frenzy is growing in interest and happening fast within the HR sector and actually with most companies in general. HR professionals are just getting started with their participation; we're basically in the infancy stage of understand how big data weaves into our daily role. These thoughts where the genesis for my research show about big data named "Thug Metrics." I'll share a quick story: again one morning over coffee the idea materialized to launch a new podcast and name it Thug Metrics; I liked an edgy named for it. You know, "thug" isn't usually related to anything HR, much less a research effort. The name was inspired by the cookbook Thug Kitchen, which has tons of excellent vegan recipes. A cookbook and Big Data in HR have nothing to do with each other, I just felt the name "Thug" was pretty cool, anyway.

Next step, I created a wish list of guests, then starting sourcing the leading experts on big data in the HR, consumer and social analytics space to discuss what they felt was significant about Big Data. I approached the question again "what's keeping you up at night" but this time about big data. Immediately several themes emerged from the conversations, giving me a research cadence to follow. One of my initial thoughts was: how will the garden-variety HR professional actually incorporate big data into their daily responsibilities? My next thought: I need more coffee—then I briefly panicked. Maybe big data will be the end of the HR function and the practitioner as we know it. Yep, I went there. I was driven to definitely go dig deeper into this whole movement called big data.

Over six months and many interviews, my data started to tell me a story. Here is what I'd set as a goal for this research journey:

a) Understand the plumbing of big data as it applies to the HR function.
b) Share what I discovered on big data with HR and those who support the HR community.

In the middle of writing the book I spoke on Big Data at a conference in Omaha, Nebraska called SocialHRCamp. The discussion with a room of HR professionals about the realities of what is important to them is amazing. Here are some thoughts from audience participants Chris Carlson and Victoria Jaeger on the question I posed: Where could big data help them in HR?

a) Adding talent and remaining the best at talent management and customer service.

b) Improving employees' misconceptions on benefits.

I'd mulled over how to present what I discovered in my interviews. My decision landed on not filtering the information or presenting my interpretation of what was most important from all the information that I'd gathered. Instead, I'm sharing the conversations as they happened in the interviews. The interview transcript in places really flows like a choppy, awkward and what seems like long-winded responses, but it's two people talking. The bonus feature if reading is not your thing is that all the interviews can be accessed online at no cost. Just Google them to find, it's how we find everything.

I definitely appreciate the experts who shared their knowledge and insights with candor and some humor about big data. I realize that everyone has hectic schedules with limited time; take just a moment to connect with our experts when you can: William Tincup, Michael Harms, Randy Roberts, Matt Gough, Jessica Miller-Merrell, Matt Charney, Steve Burton, Don MacPherson, Dr. Brent Bannon, Naomi Bloom, Ivan Casanova, David Bernstein, Jason Lauritsen, Damon Cortesi and Dr. Charles Handler.

William Tincup, Key Interval Research
Should We Trust the Data?

William is a principal analyst for Key Interval Research, a fairly new venture in the scheme of things. He's definitely one of the leading pundits of software adoption and how that suits you really well or really poorly in your organization. First of all, tell us a little bit about Key Interval Research.

Sure, and just because you are a principal doesn't mean you have principles. Just FYI. Putting that out there.

Key Interval is—the genesis of Key Interval is very simple. John Sumser and I have been consulting together for quite some time, a couple years now. We've done research for clients. We work with all software clients, and all folks who are focusing back on new recruitment, and HR market. We've done research, but we've done it quietly and we've done it behind the bale for our clients. The market has treated us for years as analysts, yet we've never really had a research function, so kind of like the caterpillar that becomes a butterfly story, at one point, you say to yourselves, ok, the market is treating you like an analyst.

You're doing research, but you're not doing publicly facing research. It's probably time for you to grow up and evolve and do this bit where you do publicly facing, so that spawned a thousand conversations between John and I, and what we are curious about is the intersections of HR and technology in particular.

Where our brethren, the Gartner, Aberdeen, IVC, Forrester, Brandon Hall, of the like, a lot of them what they do is focus on making the vendor landscape make sense. It's all crucial work; it's work that we are not doing. We are not really focused on making a landscape make sense to a practitioner. For instance, global LMS vendors, like throw a rock, how do you figure that market out? Well, there are great analyst firms that are doing that type of work. John and I are focused on behind the veil, when HR confronts technology and interacts with technology and uses technology and adopts technology, what goes on there? And there is a bunch of myths and anecdotes and facts and this that and the other all flying around, and the truth is, no one really knows. And so we are curious about that.

We've got a really aggressive research calendar for 2015. People are subscribing left and right, which is great, because they believe in John and I and they believe that we will create both great research, but also come to some really interesting and compelling recommendations. And it's all practitioner-centered.

We get this question asked of us at least once a day: is our research for the vendors or for the practitioners, and it's for practitioners. The way vendors will use this is they will get smarter in sales, marketing, and product, and it will help them in interacting with their prospects that happen to be practitioners and customers that are practitioners. So, it will make vendors smarter, no doubt about it, but really it's a game of us getting to know the HR practitioner in a more significant way as they interact with technology.

The genesis of Thug Metrics was discovering what I didn't know about Big Data through conversations with really smart people in 2015. My goal is to share insight to the practitioner to on the things that make people cringe around HR data, data intelligence, data analytics and all things predictive. Some of the nuggets and insights that can be extracted from data will maybe shared right here, right now today!

William, how do you approach the whole data intelligence question in your wheelhouse?

Absolutely. So, at Key Interval—I don't want to do this. The first thing I want to do is, I love the idea that you are going to take a year out of your life, and you're going to have conversations and learn about where we are, where we aren't, what's the future, what's the past, all that type of stuff about big data. I'm equally envious about your path and Thug Metrics and what you're going to learn from being in all kinds of compelling conversations. [Sans this one]. Of course, this one might not be as compelling, but all the other ones after this one are going to be extremely comparing, especially compared to this one.

At Key Interval, we've got two ways that we deal with data, and one way is what are the metrics and analytics that people are really using today? So, in one month, we are going to be really drilling down with 70 or so questions about, OK, cut out the myth and the facts and get right down to the heart of the matter.

You can only measure three things, what are they, etc. Because I want to know what are people really using right now because you can measure 10,000 things, and it isn't a game of whether you should measure 10,000 things. If you can, should you? And if you should, what are the ones that are going to get rolled up as the most important—and that's going to depend on the company, the industry, the size of employee head count, it's going to depend on where you sit in the organization, if you're a CHRO or the talent sourcer in a 15-person recruitment team. All those things are going to be dependent on a lot of stuff, but at the end of the day, people are measuring.

They are using measurements, they are using analytics, they are using metrics, and they have some data standards. They are doing that stuff. So, one report is going to be about what does that look like? The other is a report that is going to be looking at data models, completely different, similar, but different.

We're curious as to how do people have structured data discussions? How do people actually come to grips with what should be the data standard, what should we be collecting, and how do we test for that? How do we validate that? How do we make sure that at the end of the day, we trust the data in our own systems? So, that's kind of more of a data model line of questioning. So, we have two—we think it's so important, Bryan, that we are researching it two different ways in 2015. So, out of 12 reports, we are investing two in those to data because we think it's critical.

William, you bring up a great point. Who owns the data governance in a company?

Bryan, it used to be the CIO because it would fall under information, and information, CPO, CIO. With SaaS, HR and recruiting, it has gotten displaced, so who owns it is a question of well, who cares enough about it to be the champion. And, so far, we are not seeing that it's in HR. And it needs to be because typically, people are sitting on 13-15 different systems. Those systems don't do a great job of talking together, or with one another, and being integrated, and they have different data standards. So, it's something as simple as the payroll record is last name comma first name, and in the ATS, it's first name, last name, no commas and a space between last name and first name. And then the succession management software, it's first name no spaces comma last name. So, that's kind of a simple example of just name, and if those things don't talk, how do you ever get a real picture? So, who owns it? I don't think anyone owns it, and I think that's why we are here in the place we're at, and I think one of the discoveries you'll make along the way this year is we need the CHRO needs to be a data wizard, needs to be a data manager, needs to be a data czar, if you will.

We're sitting across the table having a drink and a cigar with someone who asks, "William, how do I get my hands around what do I want to use the data for in my company?" Where do you start with your clients?

Well, I think this is a question that keeps people up at night. What do I want to use the data for? You start at the beginning of what terrifies people about data right now is they don't trust it. Most of what is in data, and HR data in particular, is how do you fall in love with the data that you have? How do you believe it? How do you trust it so that you can make informed decisions? I think you're question is right along that, and what decisions should you be looking at, and how does data inform that?

> *"You have to go backwards, and that's the unsexy part of data right now is that it's a reclamation project. Data that moves throughout the organization, and particularly in HR, is plumbing."*
>
> —William Tincup

William, what should we measure and why?

At the end of the day, I believe that the most important metric in HR is the retention of top talent. So, a simple metric that could be used is ok, out of 1,000 person firm, here is the 80 people that are the most critical, and what is our win-loss relationship in terms of those 80 people in terms of retaining them? If we go year in and year out and we are retaining those 80, then HR is working pretty damn good. If we have a problem there, then we have a problem everywhere.

"Plumbing," I love the analogy because it's damn clever and a perfect segue. So, skilled craftsmen, the next question is: analytics itself, actually doing the analyzing of data, what's going to happen when you can't find the capabilities and the skills. William, as a practitioner you've got the question pinned down. What do you want to use the data for? Now, it's like how in the hell are we going to dive into the data with people that really know what they're doing? The massive skill gap on that, where do we go?

Bryan, first of all, anyone in HR, if you're considering a noble pursuit and a noble career in HR, take a stats class. That's the first thing. Drop-the-mic, walks off stage, and takes a stats class. They're all online and you can go to a community college, whatever it takes, take a stats class. That's where we start is we bring data literacy up. We need to up our game. Everyone in HR, anyone that hears this podcast, everyone that interacts with HR on both the working the desk as well as the people that service those folks, we need to up our game in terms of data. We need to know more about data and understand data, which means that we need to understand math and statistics and coding. So, you want to get better at it? Go take a stats class.

Second, I think that what will happen, what you and I will see in HR in the next 5 years, is the role of HR operations. And it's happened in sales. What happened is that it gave birth to this whole role is someone who is really paying attention to the math, someone that is really paying attention to conversions, someone who is really good in spreadsheets, someone who is really good working with sales force automation software, etc. We saw it happen with marketing positions. Years later, we saw it with marketing where they did the exact same thing. This isn't a true marketing position, its really marketing operations. It's someone looking at the analytics and helping us make better decisions.

HR needs to get smarter while at the same time, we are probably looking at hiring people that have that types of analyst backgrounds that understand math, can work in spreadsheets, that already come to the table with the skills that we need, and will help us. I think that's how we are going to fix it, Bryan, is that we need to get smarter on one level, that's A. B, we are going to hire people who really fill a HR operations role.

So William, to that point, do you think there is a new position created that is going to take these insights from the data and use them in transforming how the business operates?

I do. Indeed. Well, that's the role that people have been wanting. You and I both know that some of the best talent in the country around human capital, they already do that. But they have to literally piece it together to get that done, right?

Or it's not getting done at all. Worst-case scenario, it should be done. It's not getting done. It's not even getting—because we have other fires. Remember, HR, and you know this because of your interaction with HR, HR is firefighting. You come into work; you have a plan. On Sunday, you create a plan, you have an idea of what your week is going to look like, and then on Monday morning at 8AM, you show up with your Starbucks coffee, and you take that plan, and you light it on fire. You deal with what emergency is coming at you at that particular moment. You get to Friday late afternoon, and you're like wow, that week just flew by, and you didn't get to any of your plan, or you got to very little of it.

Bryan, I don't think that analytics are all that done. If they're done, they're done at the largest—the ConAgra's of the world, the Kimberly Clarks of the world. They probably have whole teams that are doing nothing but pour through this type of data. OK, fair enough. Those guys, yeah. They've got analytics pretty much handled. For everyone else that isn't ConAgra, not so much.

We all know that people quit because of bad managers. They don't quit bad companies; they quit bad managers. What if in your analysis you find, for sure, with certainty, that Bob is a terrible manager? Oh, by the way, Bob has been there the longest. He is the longest tenured employee, and he's beloved. Everyone else loves him, unless you work for him, they hate his guts. Everyone else thinks he's a terrible manager. Do you really fire Bob? Really? Most people would say no. They would get that data and they would say, no way in Hell we can fire Bob. Nope. Now what do we do?

You're absolutely right. The data can tell you something you don't want to know because it's really nice to have your head in the sand and not know, but I think those days are coming to an end, and I really do believe that the transparency that you and I are confronting on a daily basis, those folks are going to have no where to hide, and we are going to have to deal with the Bobs of the world. We are going to have to just deal with it, and grow up, quite frankly.

William, how far behind do you feel that the human capital function is relative to data from marketing?

It's behind at least 10 years and probably closer to 15 years. Given my experience in marketing, we were talking about these same things in 1998 in marketing and advertising. So, the return on advertising, the discussions of the J. Walker Thompson and Ogilvy of the world was a 95-98 discussion. You know that I mean? And people have said this often, and they have said it about HCM in particular behind the world of CRM.

What happened in CRM about 10 years ago is about what is happening for us, so it's behind, and it doesn't really matter how far behind. The thing is, we can learn a lot about marketing and how they went through it and they are on the other side of it. You talk to a marketer today, and they are quick to pull out a spreadsheet on you, they are quick to talk about analytics. They know how to create pivot tables. They are just comfortable. You can't have an art discussion with a marketer anymore. Gone are those days. I've been in conversations with marketers recently, and I'm like, you know, it's the difference between Manet and Monet, and they have no idea what I'm talking about. And part of me hates that because as a marketer you should know something about art. At least from my perspective, you should know something about art.

So, I don't want to lose that in HR. We are in the people business. We are people, and that's not something you want to run away or shy from. That's really a good thing, that's what makes us human, and I don't want to squeeze the humanity out of human resources. So, I want to take all the good things out of technology and data, but I don't want to lose our humanity in the process.

William, what was the tipping point, like in the marketing advertising function; that they really dug into analytics?

Bryan, they were forced at gunpoint, just like HR. They were forced because it was about budget. It was about dollars and budget. So, they had to get quote on quote smarter around what was working and what wasn't. So, the analytics back then, you had to know, you've only got $100,000 in budget, where do you spend the money? You've got to know return. And so, ROI became—it's a zero sum game. If you put $10,000 toward this expenditure, you have $90,000 left, so now what? So, they were really forced at gunpoint to become more analytics oriented, but it was all around budget. In HR, I don't know it's all around budget. I think its people looking at us to make business decisions based on data. So, data-driven business decisions, if you will. I think people are looking to HR to do that, but I don't think it's as closely tied to budget as it was in marketing.

William is there any external data that piques your interest within the human capital and HR function that you could potentially pipe in, overlay it, and make you go "huh"?

Yeah, I think customer data. Anytime you can get customer data and pull out customer data, even if it's ratings data from a Trip Advisor or Glassdoor or anything that's outside that can give you some customer data. There is nuance stuff, like in healthcare, tying it to patient satisfaction. So, having all the HR data over here, and then over here, you have this thing that drives most healthcare establishments, patient satisfaction, and bringing those together. Bringing those data sources together and overlaying, I think will yield great results. In the restaurant sector, you're looking for customer satisfaction. At the tabletop, you want to know who is doing well at the table top, and how does that relate to performance data? You see performance management software, and how does it inform compensation succession and other things, so I think every industry is probably going to have nuanced stuff.

I don't think it's going to be just everybody should have these five data points; I think it depends on the industry. You want to look outside of HR for other types of data that you can bring to HR. And vice versa, where we can port data to them as well.

Last question William. Social sensing. Where do you pull in social behaviors and social data? Where is that going to put the most amount of pressure on overall data, kind of data intelligence?

On some level, the comment of publicly praised, privately criticized, I think that has been a rule that has been around for 1000 years-ish. I don't think that changes. I don't think that because you connect someone's Twitter feed to his or her performance management data, I don't think that's necessarily a bad thing. It's just what are you going to get? Ripple did this years ago, where they basically said performance reviews suck, and oh by the way, they are social, or they should be social. You know, I could kind of see that. That's going to draw out a lot of positivity, but no one is going to go in there—or no one probably should go in there because it is going to be career limiting—go in there and be really critical. I mean, again, if you're going to be critical, you're probably going to do that privately. You're not going to go out on Facebook and say I love my boss, but dot-dot-dot give them criticism because to do so means you probably won't have a job there, at least you will be very limited.

So, I think looking at social data is like where can it inform, where can we use the mediums of social data to deliver messages to an audience? I think Global Force does a really good job of this on the recognition side. Where they look at that data and say you want to thank somebody, they give you a couple options. Do you want to thank them privately, do you want to send an email, do you want to thank them via social, and it becomes kind of another outlet, if you will, for that message. I kind of like that. I think there is something to that.

I think we've both seen people that do social background checks. Again, where do these worlds overlay? I think that's savvy. I think there are multiple products, but I know TalentWise has a product where it's a background check, but in this particular background check, they monitor your social footprint, and then come back and grade your social footprint.

Bryan, let's be honest, I'm unemployable. Anyone grading my social footprint, I'm not really worried about that. However, there are a whole lot of people who aren't like me, and they do care deeply, and they would like to know what people think about their social footprint. If you're looking for ways there social and HR data interact, I think there are a bunch. We are on the very front-end of that wave. So, there's going to be more to come. We shouldn't have our heads in the sand. We should look at social data just like we look at customer data or sales data or patient satisfaction data. We should bring it in when it makes sense.

Michael Harms, TDn2K

The Dawn of Analytics

Welcome Michael Harms, the Executive Director of Operations from TDn2K based in Dallas, Texas.

Thanks Bryan, as you mentioned I work for a Dallas-based company. We're kind of a niche analytics firm, and we have been in this game for 20 years. Just celebrating our 20th anniversary, so we have been around for a while doing this. We like to joke that we're not into big data so much as medium-sized data. But again, at the end of the day, numbers are numbers, math is math, data is data, and again, there is a lot of application to this, uses for it, and it's kind of interesting to watch the new uses of technology develop what you can do with some of the information that wasn't available 20 years ago, and how it is coming of age and people are taking a new interest in data analytics.

What we do is we focus on service sector companies, and we help analyze and benchmark their performance against each other. So, we get companies to aggregate their data under the veil of privacy that we provide, and we help them make sense of how they are performing relative to similar types of organizations. And we do that on both human resources metrics, performance and financial analytics, and we are delving into the social space as well. So, it's kind of evolved from a much simpler and smaller data set to a much more robust platform and what we can do as well.

Michael, first question that comes to mind is, is variety or volume of data more important?

Bryan, Wow. That's a good question. You know, just to put a qualifier on everything, I guess it depends. Obviously, the more volume you have, often the more confidence you have in what you are reporting. It gives you a wider spectrum to see the outliers of what constitutes the norm. At the same time, one data point, or one element doesn't always tell the story. We live in a multivariable world. So, that's a really interesting question, but I like to have both. I like to have my hands on as much as I can get of both, and then we can make sense of it. Obviously, there are certain data points, depending on what you are looking at, that are more important than others, but that's really an interesting way to look at it. I think that what we're seeing is that over the past few years we've seen really a fire-hose of information get turned on from a trickle, and the ability to transport and protect this information has made the volume issue a really big deal, and how you handle that volume of information. There's a lot of new technology out there that is exciting and frightening at the same time. But yeah, I think the volume is definitely important, but at the end of the day, you've got to be looking at the right things.

Lets go a little further in that stream of thought, internal versus external data, and how you would intersect those and make that into something worthwhile. What is the thought process as you talk to your clients and you think about it personally as you are jumping into these big, multivariable sets of data.

Well, that's another interesting dilemma that we often face is, sometimes the macro information is boring to people, but yet it is very important. When you can start marrying that micro data with the macro data is sometimes where you find some really interesting things. Especially if you are talking about the business world, and economic development, business performance, stuff like that, where there is a clear correlation between the macro economic performance; that external data, which everyone has access to, or even the social space. People's comments are out there for everyone to see, and what does that mean? And that's where you really get into that interesting space because we're living in that micro, or customized, world.

We really want to know what's going on at a very granular level, and I think that's where we've gotten into this interesting space, with the new technology, the new tools, that we can use some of that, and often that is internal information. You tie it to that external information, and you look for things that matter. And I think that's really the crux of all of the big data, or just the metrics and analytics, is tell me what matters. We're collecting this information. You have all this new data, new tools at your disposal, and your goal is to make sense of the world and what is going on.

Bryan, the point of this is to kind of step back, and figure out what is going on. I think at the end of the day, everybody wants predictability. Whether it's in business, or life, the weather, the stock market, relationships, just as people, we crave predictability and foresight, so we know what to expect. No one likes to be caught off guard. Again, that's the point of analyzing all this information, is to sort the stuff that is interesting from the stuff that matters, and the stuff that people will pay for if you're a business and you're relying on this to put food on your table.

Michael, you brought up social, kind of the new layer of social data. These social platforms, social technology and social media in general; how does social censing and that whole layer of data that's now really it's personal consumer data that is really putting pressure and insight and it's taking the dimension of how you can look at your business and behaviors and flip it on its head.

How is that affecting your sector? Because you're a service sector, a hospitality sector of business, so I would assume it's gigantic, but still fairly in its infancy. So, how is it affecting you guys? How should we be thinking about it?

To give everyone a better idea, we deal with a lot of restaurants. Their performance and how they are doing. Obviously, there are a lot of restaurants and now when people have a platform to say how they feel about their meal or their service, or they are taking pictures and posting them on Instagram, there are just reams of information and feedback for operators that they didn't have just a few years ago. The scale has just exponentially exploded. So again, making sense of what does it mean when someone takes a picture of their cheeseburger or their dessert if they make a comment on Twitter or Facebook, how do you translate that to was it a good thing? Was this a bad thing? How did this reflect in my performance? Does this reflect poorly on the service they received? The food quality? There are a million factors you can really read from this. So, kind of trying to read the tea leaves, and we are really at the starting point of doing that, and we all like to think we've got it figured out, but it really is an interesting new dawn in this art and science of trying to glean the proper feedback, and again, what it means.

Bryan, you're getting that feedback at a micro level. We're really looking to figure out, what are the correlations between some of that feedback and both the volume, and what they are talking about. So, it really is kind of an interesting new day for that sort of analysis, and we are just kind of getting our feet wet in that and seeing where it takes us.

Michael, is the speed because obviously social data is coming in—it's real and raw, and—what considerations do you think about or should we be thinking about to deal with that type of data versus everything else in the business sector that's usually not real time?

Bryan, it's usually put through, you know, set up in a matrix of question and answer-type matrix that you are pulling from, whether it's point of sale, or whatever the case may be.

How does social data work—does it get treated differently?

Bryan, again "Wow" you're spot on there. I think the speed is very important because we are really moving toward a call and response world. You hear the buzzword, the Internet of things. I hate that term, but again, that customized world we are living in, and you think about the nest thermostat, where it kind of learns when you turn the heat on or off or when you're away or when you're hot, and then it can preempt your temperature variability there. When you can make it second nature, that's great, but when you're dealing with a giant mass of consumers who are all giving you feedback, it gets a little trickier. That's where everybody wants it. They want that call and response where someone comments, and you can respond to it immediately. Like, you did not like your service, you did not like the way you were treated, or something disappointed you, you can respond to it on the fly, and that's where Twitter has become a huge platform from airlines to basically any customer-facing enterprise, can get feedback immediately via Twitter. It's just a matter of handling the volume and seeing what that means.

Bryan, I feel the other thing you have to deal with is people may be more prone to voice their displeasure than to voice their pleasure on some of these platforms. So you've got to take that into consideration as well when you are trying to decipher what some of this means. But I do think the speed and the immediacy of both the feedback and how the customer can respond to the feedback, that's really a game changer. You know, if someone does something to upset you, and you are able to respond to that immediately and show that their happiness does matter to you, that makes a lot bigger difference than if you get an I'm sorry 6 weeks down the road after it is filtered through a few layers of bureaucracy. So, I think the speed is another one of those game changers along with the volume.

Data governance, who has historically has owned data, data analysis in organizations, and is that changing Michael? Do you see it changing in the future way down the road? There are three questions there, by the way.

Bryan, I do think it has changed, and again, different companies, different industries, we have the pleasure of working with a lot of different companies of various size, and what's really fascinating is that you see companies that place a lot of emphasis on data and internal systems and companies that don't value it as much. So, again, that's kind of personal taste of management style. Maybe some of it is transition, maybe some of it is just resources that they have at their disposal. At the end of the day, though, we are seeing a general trend where the IT teams are becoming more and more robust when it comes to this. They are designing a lot more systems, companies are implementing more systems; we're seeing more chief technology officers than we have ever seen before.

We are seeing companies starting to develop analytic teams, that their sole purpose is to analyze information from both internal and external resources, marrying them together. It's been a really quick change that we have seen over I'd say the last 5 or 6 years. I think that's going to continue to develop, and the companies that don't follow along that pattern are going to find they're falling behind. I think that there has been a clear change, a renewed emphasis on the importance of information and metrics and analytics, because again, they do really help you run your company better. So, what was the second question?

Oh, I think you answered all three in one fell swoop. Michael, that was an awesome total-answer.

Michael, ok, where can data go horribly wrong for companies? And then I'm going to give you the big question, let's think for a second, and then I'm also going to get into the data security question, all in the news with Hollywood, and Sony pictures, and foreign governments. Data, big data, data security, is a big topic at the moment. So, we'll start out with the little question, and then we'll move on to the big question.

"Lies, damned lies, and statistics."

—Phrase popularized by Mark Twain (among
others), attributed to the 19th-century
British Prime Minister Benjamin Disraeli
(1804–1881)

Bryan, well first of all, where data can go wrong, I think it was the famous Mark Twain quote that gets bandied about all the time about lies, damn lies, and statistics. I think that sometimes companies look at the metrics, look at the data, and they don't like what they see. It's like owning a scale, and you stand on it every morning and you don't like the number, so you stop using the scale. I think that's one way in which companies can go wrong if they just stop using it because they don't like the output or maybe they've got bonuses tied to performance, and the performance isn't what they want it to be. So, you know, shoot the messenger. That's one way.

I think the other one is, and I think this is one that everybody on both sides of the table need to be careful of, is just that hubris I would say. Just because you have some insight, you have that information, you have these tools—the dawn of analytics, the day of this has come—we think that we have this information and it makes us God. That we know have all the answers, and the numbers don't lie. You've got to be very wary of that. One of the things we say, when we are collecting data on this scale, is garbage in garbage out, right? If there is something wrong with the information that you are looking at, then the decisions that you make or the output that you get is going to be very flawed, and we see this a lot too.

You've got to be very careful about what you're looking at, and you have to have a strong confidence in what you're looking at, and just be grounded enough to realize that it's a tool and it's going to give you some insight, some predictability, some foresight, but it's not the be all, end all. So, just remaining grounded when you're looking at this often helps as well.

Bryan, when you're talking about the security component, it's a frightening world out there. I just read an article in the Wall Street Journal that references the Internet of things, and they felt like 2014 was when that came to fruition. More and more devices were connecting to the internet, that information is being shared, and while it has some amazing possibilities there for making life better for all of humanity, there is also some terrifying aspects of that because that information is just out there, and if you have some determined hackers, they are going to get to that information somehow, someway. As we become more and more reliant on automated systems for our power and water supply, and how we run our businesses, and our personal information, our health information.

Again, the possibility exists that there are repercussions to that that could really come back to bite us in the end. It's kind of frightening. We've seen what has happened with Sony, and with Home Depot and Target, and a lot of these companies with credit card transactions. You start thinking about if it's your water supply, or your electrical grid, or if you've got a self-driving car, there are a lot of scary things that could happen. Even on a much smaller scale, if you're a business, and you have intellectual property or private information, the fact that there are people out there who are nosing around for it, it's a little disconcerting, and I think most of those companies that are in this space take it very seriously.

We feel like we have an ethical and moral obligation to do the right thing with that information. I know sometimes, that kind of gets cast by the wayside in the capitalist system, but I think there has been renewed interest in making sure we are doing the right thing with some of that information, and you have seen more and more people get uncomfortable with that. Some people are saying- I don't want Google with all my information. It makes me a little uneasy. What are they doing with that? So, I think there is a large onus on the people doing the data collecting and doing the analysis because again, there's a scary new world out there.

Michael, you ready for this one? What is your favorite algorithm?

My favorite algorithm, Bryan, I don't even know how to answer that. I will say because I am old school, with all the new tools out there, I always like it when people dis your basic Excel file because I'm like, to me, that was a game changer. Excel changed the world for us. People see it as a spreadsheet, it's really like a rudimentary coding language the way I see it. If you know what you're doing, you can write some mean formulas. I've always joked, I could build a robot in Excel. Some of your basic stuff, it's pretty cool if you know what you're doing.

Great answer! That's a pretty tough question.

Michael. What are some of the top challenges you see in 2015 for starting to look and analyze and use the intelligence from data?

Well, I think one of the big challenges is, again, companies are becoming more and more comfortable looking at data and looking at the analytics. Some of them have added new staff to handle this and help their operations and management teams. Some people just kind of adapting and changing with the times, but everybody is becoming a little more technologically savvy, and data savvy. I think that's a good thing. It also presents a new realm of challenges because there is the opportunity to misinterpret things, and people are wanting; things more and more defined on a micro level. Again, that trend of ok, that's what's going on in the United States, or that's what's going on in California or Texas, what's going on in this zip code or on this block or you know, they really want that targeted, and that's something new for us. We've always knew that was coming, but for it to come this fast, and for more and more people asking for information that is just so specifically targeted.

Again, when you mention about the volume of data, when you have 20 years of information to analyze, you get a feel for what's right and what's wrong on a larger scale. This is kind of a new thing for us to look at it on this micro scale. Making sure your trust level is where it needs to be and your confidence level that you are reporting things that are accurate, especially if they are going to be making decisions based on this, that's a new challenge for us because it's something we haven't done. It's new to us as well, and I think a lot of companies are finding that, that the volume and the tools have allowed them to do things they've never done before.

Listen Bryan; you want to make sure you are doing the right thing and that you're absolutely confident that you are looking at and the decisions that you are making.

One of the challenges that I definitely see is that when dealing with data in the modeling and anywhere from setting up asking the right questions to looking at the data to creating some actionable things that you can do with the data, that's all very math-intensive. So, the skill gap for data scientists, the number of them, and the people who are really good at that, it's kind of like developers, like mobile developers. Hard to find, it's scarce and scarcer all the time. That, to me, is the single biggest threat to the new era of data is people that are really good at doing the analysis. Doing the heavy lifting on the math.

> *"The single biggest threat to the new era of data is people that are really good at doing the analysis. Doing the heavy lifting on the math."*
>
> —MICHAEL HARMS

Yeah Michael, I would agree with that.

Bryan, we like to joke at our company that—I work with some really smart people, and you might say this person is in the top 1% in IT development, or this person is in the top 1% in math and analytical capability, but the difference between the top 0.1% within that 1%, that is leaps and bounds, and again, those people that are just absolutely brilliant are few and far between. The rest of us have to do. Us mere mortals like you and me.

Bryan, I feel that, again, some of the technology is the great equalizer, but I've always said that math, to me, is a universal language. It's the language of business. It transports across cultures and continents, and if you want to speak the language of business, you have to understand what numbers mean, whether that's a balance sheet, or whether that's in metrics and analytics. We're seeing that now more than ever.

Randy Roberts, formerly HP

C.I.A. (Confidentiality, Integrity, and Availability)

Randy Roberts, formerly of HP is CEO and Founder of Digital Security Advisors. Randy, welcome to the show.

Hi, Bryan, and thanks for having me on today.

What a perfect time to talk about digital security, data security, cyber security. That question is going to come up a little later on about what the hell that all means. So, if you would, tell us a little bit about your background and what your company does.

Sure, Bryan. My company is Digital Security Advisors. It's a company that I founded and what we do is we provide advice to people about how to properly secure their digital assets. We provide some seminars on how to do that kind of work.

So, my background, I started Digital Security Advisors and prior to that, I was employed with Hewlett-Packard, HP. At HP I was a network security manager. I managed a global team of people that did our day-to-day operational stuff to keep a large number of firewalls and network intrusion prevention systems operating. I did a lot with our guys that ran our systems that the analysts use to look at the data coming off those devices. A typical security analyst is who looking at intrusions and trying to figure out what to do next. I worked a lot with our people that did more the research once we knew we had an intrusion and we bring in our team, who did all the response to that, worked with those guys on responses. It was a very interesting job I had with HP, I really enjoyed it.

Another piece I worked with at HP and in my role as a network security manager, is I spent a lot of time with architects looking at what are we going to do for the future? How are we going to build our networks out, how is that going to work? Prior to HP, I spent a number of years with EDS. As you know, HP bough EDS back in 2008 when I was in that transition, I was actually working within the global information security position within EDS, doing basically advisory services then to various internal and external teams on how to properly do network security, how to do network security policy, and general security policy. So, I've been doing the network security stuff since about 2004, and it's been a real interesting time to be engaged in this stuff, and I've really enjoyed it quite a bit.

Randy, there's a lot of terminology that gets thrown around. Different industries have different jargon and different slants on it, so I know you've got digital security, cyber security, and data security. What are the differences for those terms and what that all means?

Well, Bryan, I hear a lot of terms. There's also just general IT security. The reality is that all of them pretty much deal with the same thing, and that is how are we going to properly secure our digital assets, whether that is our data, our networks, and our application. And then within that whole umbrella of IT security, we look at different skill sets, different tools, and different mechanisms for how we execute that security. But really, I don't think anyone could give you a good difference between what is different between data security versus cyber security. I think those terms are just thrown around a lot. I like the term IT security just because it covers everything.

Got it, well that's good to know. So, now that I hear all that, I guess cyber security is the sexiest of the terms. That's probably why that's been more adopted by pop culture as the thing to look at. If you can bill more by calling it cyber security, then I think you should call it cyber security.

Bryan, we see that term a lot more in the government space. If you go look for jobs that are government-related, there are a lot of cyber jobs. If you look at the government contractors, a lot of them are cyber, but if you get outside of those spaces, it's more general IT security.

Interesting. Well, that's a very tangible difference, too. If you could, kind of distill down into more consumable bites, what data security actually means. Just for the average business owner or even technical professional who doesn't deal with the security side. Give us some framework to think about cyber security since that's a gigantic term.

Yeah, it is a gigantic term, and even those of us who do this for a living will tell you, it covers so much. But the bottom line is that we have so much of our stuff in some form of digital format. Whether that is something we see stolen all the time, like credit card data, but it also is not just that. It's also business plans, it's spreadsheets, which have highly confidential data in it. Basically, think of anything that is of value to your or your company that is in a digital form, and typically we want to know who is looking at that, and why are they looking at it. Should they be looking at it is the real question. Should someone be able to have access to that data?

Let's go back 30-40 years ago. All that data, for the most part, was on paper. We stuck it in a file cabinet, and we gave the right person the key to that file cabinet. You knew hey, George has the key to that thing, and George and his guys or his gals are the only people who can get to it. Today, that stuff exists on a hard drive someplace, and the question you still have to ask is it only George and his people who can get to it, or can anybody on the network get to it? And if your network is connected to the Internet, can anyone in the world get to it who is connected to the

Internet? Those kinds of questions begin to drive the concepts around IT security. Then, we look at we don't want everyone in the world to see it, how do we construct our system so that only the right people can see it? Bottom line that is what this is all about. That's the primary thing.

If you look at the typical, if you go out there and you do a search for IT security Bryan, you'll see this term used a lot. CIA. CIA is just an acronym for confidentiality, integrity, and availability. Those concepts are fairly clear. Confidentiality means that only the right people see something. That's what I was talking about earlier. Integrity is has somebody messed with your data? We see that too. Think of websites where the old thing back in the 90s was people loved deface websites, so they'd go in and put somebody's other stuff up. We saw it with Sony. This GOP gang went out and put up stuff on Sony's website, so when you accessed the Sony website, you got this nasty message about how horrible Sony was. So, the integrity of their website was messed with. So, that's the piece of that. A is availability, and A is the piece that most IT folks are extremely familiar with. When your application is not working; phones ring, and it's usually phone calls from people who just want to yell at you and get it fixed. So, confidentiality, integrity, and availability; when we are dealing with security, we want to make sure that all of those things match up with the requirements that are needed for them to the data that is being stored, the system that is being used, the application that is available. Does that make sense at a big picture level?

Randy, absolutely, I just recently listening to a data interview with a global expert, and he put it into really simple terms that I liked. He said: if you're a global company, and your front door is not working, you can't lock it, everybody's not going to go home and leave the front door unlocked. It's going to get fixed. Before anyone leaves, it's going to get fixed. It's going to be monitored and it's going to get fixed. Why can't that be the same with your digital front lines? And I thought that was incredibly—he distilled it down to the simple, day to day—you know, you don't leave your house or you don't leave your car with the doors wide open. Letting everybody in, you don't care. You just don't do that. Why do you do it with your digital assets? I thought that was really articulated in an easy way that I understood and that I remembered.

Bryan to build on that real work analogy, the real issue is, if I work for a company that has a fleet of vehicles, and I run the yard, the fleet yard, I walk out into my fleet yard when I get there in the morning, and I can look out and count the number of vehicles out there, and typically look and say they are all here. Most of us—I mean, you can hire anyone to go and run that kind of a count. It's not real hard to look out there, count the number of cars, and tell me if I have all of them there. Now, when I ask you to go do that, though, for your records in your database, or the number of files that exist of a particular type on your primary system, we go from everybody being able to do that to just a few people being able to do that. Typically, people with very specific training, and we've made something that seems pretty simple much more complex. The number of people that can do that is much smaller. The tools that you have to do that with aren't quite as easy. I mean, write down a number, check or whatever. It's simple in the real world. It's very complex in the digital world. The other thing is, I can go count all my digital records and say yep, they're all there, but I don't know that someone hasn't taken a perfect copy of them and moved them somewhere else.

So, I know if someone has taken a car out of my fleet. It's very obvious. You can't just make a perfect copy of it and leave one there for me, but with digital records, it is extremely hard because that's exactly what happens. People take perfect copies, they move them somewhere else, and they've got the exact same thing to work from that you've got. So, the act of securing stuff in the digital space takes skill and expertise that we'd normally think of, and so, it also requires different ways to think about things. Also, just because I've got everything doesn't mean I haven't lost everything at the same time. So, it's a fascinating area to work, where we've got some very interesting problems to solve, and some of them are not clear to the average person who is doing work because of the different issues that come along with how digital works, and how easy it is to make accurate copies of everything you do with very little effort.

Randy, are you up to date on the JP Morgan breach? I know the article was in the New York Times this morning.

I haven't seen that article Bryan. I have read some about that hack, and it's kind of fascinating to me. There's a number of issues that happened there, but quite often, there are certain things that happen in our industry that just seem to happen again and again and again. One of the things that I've read about in relationship to JP Morgan is that their patch cycles were way too long, so, they were getting notified by their vendors that they needed to do updates, and they were not getting those updates applied in time, and that causes real problems.

We used to do all this—I remember, we go back 15 years, and it was real common to get a vendor update, and we'd have to run them through exhaustive testing to figure out is it going to work well within our ecosystem. I think a lot of people still have that kind of mindset about things. The problem is, today, especially for anything that is Internet connected, by the time the vendor puts out the patch, the malware guys are deconstructing what happened there. They are reverse engineering stuff, and they are putting together malware that will take advantage of that. Typically, within hours, it used to be weeks, but now it is within hours. They can figure out what changed in this piece of code that Microsoft or Oracle or Google or somebody just distributed, and they can gen up the code to make use of that. Then, they start their scanning or they go to their previous scans and they see where is this code implemented today? Where is this version of this code implemented today, they can start known implementations and get good results.

I suspect if you are a bank, you're a huge target already just because that's where the money is. That hasn't changed from the days of the old guys when they said why do you rob banks; because that's where the money is. That hasn't changed. The methodology for robbing a bank has changed. So I would suspect there are tools out there where I can scan the available stuff from a bank, and find out what kind of software they are running in their environment. Now, if I was running a team of people who were out there doing bad, I would be looking at banks with that kind of a mindset, where I would scan them on a regular basis just to see what they are doing. When Microsoft or Oracle or Google comes out with a new piece of code and says here's the issue, I would be able to know that Bank XYZ is vulnerable until they get this patch. So, I think that is the way our malware economy works today. Those people do that. They have automated their technology, they have gotten very good at it, very good at scripting. And, so when we leave doors open, they just knock them down and get in. They have proven that again and again and again and again.

So, if you're patch cycles aren't lightning fast, there are issues. Believe me, there are all kinds of problems with that because we go back to our previous point about the CIA conversation, the A being availability. Often, these patches impact availability, and often people are not tolerant enough about the need to be down for 5 minutes so they can do patching on a regular basis. So, there is a huge conflict within organizations. Do I patch, or do I wait? Do I test more to make sure it's not going to cause problems when I patch? And sometimes, in certain organizations, they spend too much time in the analysis piece, and as a result, they have left themselves wide open for a period of time, and someone takes advantage of it. I think that goes back to our job as security people are to make sure things like that don't happen. We have to have louder voices, we have to have professional voices talking with our management, and often that means way high up Board of Directors type stuff. This is mission critical and business critical and it is just as important as staying up, providing that availability, is getting it so it is patched so it is not insecure.

Randy, is part of this also just about the skill and knowledge and training of people actually on the job working in those companies?

Oh yeah Bryan, I think that's a huge part of it. I should be clear. There are not enough people doing security out there. There are just not enough. You can read all kinds of things out there in what's going on in that space, and the experts will tell you, we just don't have enough people to do the work. Part of that is a skills issue, part of that is just a—although it pays well, quite frankly, it can be quite a grind as a career, and it's just not as sexy as other stuff. You go write an application and sell the heck out of it and make a lot of money, you're doing security, you're basically fighting every day for people to get—I think there are some incentive issues for bringing people into this side of the business. There is also the fact that the best guys at security are typically really good at other things too. It takes a lot of skill to be good at this, and there is a lot of different ways a person can make a living today without the kind of grind you have to go through with the stuff that goes on with security, quite frankly. So, most people who are doing this really love it. That's the good side of it. The people who are in it really love it, and the people who are in it, for the most part, are pretty good at it. They get weeded out pretty quick if they're not. So, I think there is an issue.

Do we have enough people doing it? No. Are the people doing it skilled enough? For the most part, I would say they are, but they need help. They just need more people that can help do what they do.

Where does mobile figure into this Randy? How has that changed, or has that changed the landscape that you deal with on a daily basis?

It's huge, Bryan. I think the simple reality is that the cell phone that I carry today is better than the laptop I had 6 years ago. It's got more power, it's got more memory, and it's just an amazing device. Mobile brings its own huge set of problems. We are really dependent upon, if we go back to just 10 years ago; we are dependent on Microsoft for security. Thank God they are much better than they used to be. In the last 15 years, they have gone from being horrible to being really good. I mean, today they are really good. They do good stuff. But today, I'm dependent upon Apple being good, I'm dependent on Google being good, I'm dependent upon a few other minor players being good. And then I'm dependent upon all these application writers being good at what they do too.

The reality is we've got so much data on our phones today; it's really kind of scary when you get right down to it. And it's my phone. Most people feel like it's my phone. Even though I signed this little deal and put some other software on there so I can connect to a company's network, it's still my phone. And yet, I've got data on there that is really company proprietary stuff, and is really important to the company. So, we've got a conflict about whose phone is it? What can I do on it? What can I not do on it? Most of us agree that the company can wipe our phone if we lose them. Sometimes that happens, even when we don't use them. People get really pissed about that when their phone gets wiped, and they had their baby pictures on it, and didn't back it up.

There's all kinds of issues with that that we didn't have when, you know, I had a laptop, it was owned by the company, the company procured it, bought it, they paid for the asset, they gave it to me, and it was mine to use, but it was really clear whose device that was. It was the companies. Mobile is just so much more personal, and quite frankly, the technology is also much newer, so it creates some issues. Even though the devices are extremely powerful, we don't see the same security applications on them that we used to see on our laptop and desktop devices; although, there are really good security applications to be used in the mobile space. Security in the mobile space grew up in many of the apps. So, there is this huge problem just from a usability perspective. People just want their phones to be their phones and do all the stuff they want to do on them. They want to be able to download apps and have fun and do neat things with them, and yet, the companies want to be able to control them and do them securely, and it presents some huge challenges.

Bryan, as an industry we have gotten some solutions that have begun to get quite good, but quite frankly, I think we've still got a long way to go there, and a lot of work to do. More on the—I mean, there is the technical side of the security, definitely has room for improvement there, but then that whole aspect of the social thing that happens when I believe it's my device, and I am just using it for convenience in my company versus the company device and the company can…so there are some interesting problems there that are both technical and not technical that have to be solved for us to get to a good place with security on it.

I'll ask you, Bryan, a question on this because I'm pretty certain you carry a smartphone, and the question would be how good do you feel about having your company data on your phone? Do you feel secure with that?

Randy, I probably feel too secure. I've got my little four digit code, but relative to the lengths of security—I have an iPhone, so I probably feel even more secure, which could be completely false because I've never fact-checked it, but needless to say, I don't have the level of confidence that I do with my Linksys router, and my laptop, my Mac. I don't have the layers of proven that I can see technology on there and mobile phones are an interesting thing. I try to do everything. I try and keep everything in the cloud, and I do a couple different ways, and I use strong passwords, of course, but I keep everything in the cloud, which is a whole other approach—we could do a whole show on how the cloud has changed the landscape.

So, that's probably my final question Randy for the show is, what has the cloud done to your world as far as digital security?

Well, it's done a lot because as an individual user, I love the cloud. As a guy doing stuff in security, I'm awfully wary of it. As a guy running a small business, I love it. It's driven my cost down. My gosh; the ability to do what we do in a cloud today and the ability to get what we get for the prices we pay is just incredible. But I'm very wary about what's going on from a security perspective there, and I think we see that with a lot of companies. I know when I was at HP, we sold a lot of clouds, and it was private clouds. If you go into a Fortune 500 company, in most cases, I would say to those guys, you're crazy to use a cloud. You need enough horsepower within your own environment to do it yourself, so throw your own racks of servers up. Put the right operating system on there. Put in the cloud and learn to use that because you're going to need those management facilities anyway, and as you grow, you can then start to effectively manage a cloud within your own environment and learn the tools and skills you need to be able to secure that, which will then translate into how do you have the conversation with a cloud provider so that you can get what you need out of it. I mean, the security out there is just frightening in some respects, but that's the way it is.

The bottom line with cloud security is who owns that data. When someone shows up and asks that provider; I want access to that. Is that your call or is it their call? If it's their call, you just lost your CIA, right? You've lost your confidence, your integrity, and your availability. So you have to be careful about that. The cloud's a big deal, a great way to save money. It's not clear it's good for security at this point.

Matt Gough, Echovate
Predict This, Big Data

Welcome Matt Gough, Chief Echovator at Echovate. Tell us a little bit about yourself and about your company real quick to get us started.

I'm an entrepreneur that's been at this for a while. I started when I had a lot more hair on my head, and this is my fourth venture, Echovate, and we have a really cool platform that we've developed. It's a data driven talent analytics platform, and essentially what we do is we compile and unify existing data sets from all around the web, and we layer those on top of the foundation of data science and through our patent pending science algorithms, we are able to, in real time, from the cloud, from any mobile device, help an organization understand the impact that a candidate is going to have on their organization. Are they a good fit for the position, for the culture, and most importantly, is how does all of that ties to the overall growth, health, and improvement in revenue for that organization.

Matt, I feel one of the biggest areas that we have the ability to really make an impact within operational efficiencies and actually on business, is the talent function. The people function within companies using data. Using data intelligence to make decisions.

Bryan, Absolutely.

What are your thoughts on that Matt?

I mean, I think that, 20 years ago, this conversation wouldn't happen because obviously the Internet and all the data that is out there, 90 percent of the data information on the Internet has been built and published and put out there in the last two, two and a half years. So, it's this really interesting time in history where we have all this data, the technology is available to mash it up, bring it together, to use it in a really sophisticated, intelligent way to move business forward, you know, to make people's jobs and lives easier, and I think overall, time spent more valuable.

Matt, one of the things that sit across all functions of the business is data, because of the technology advances and just the overall philosophy around how to manage business; every single function now has data available. I feel the cloud has made people think about it in a more centralized way, versus having everything silo'd and we can't share that because there's some kind of potential negative.

Bryan, You know, what's nice about it too, is I think that with data, you are able to, in certain business functions anyway, you are able to remove maybe some of the bias, maybe some of the emotional aspects of it. I remember my first business. We used to call it fact-founded decision making. The reality is now with data, you can use that as sort of a central source to base your decisions on. Not that you have to do everything based on data because obviously there is a human element, but I think it's an important foundation to make really sound, educated, thought-through, obviously data driven decisions, and I think in doing that, it creates this really sort of grand consistency across an organization, and even across, you know, across a country like the United States where it helps us be more competitive and, you know, do great things.

Matt, what is your definition of big data?

I don't even call it big data; personally I just call it data. I think big data is more, it's turned into more of a buzzword and I hesitate to say that when I'm having conversations with people. But you know, really what it is is these really large, massive datasets that are out there, or inside companies, and you can analyze them computationally to look at patterns, trends, associations of different things. It's data. The nice thing is that it's not 20 data points; it can be 20 million or 2 billion data points. So, for me Bryan, the definition of it is that it's everything that's out there is data. I mean, we can look at things like the price of oil, we can look at things, how far somebody lives from the office, and we can look at things around what the current economic trends are looking like. Those are all data that goes into this mosaic, you know, to analyze and to try to make some sort of substantial, statistically valid decisions.

Let's talk about that data intelligence first and then the follow-up question will be for the smallest organizations without resources.

Bryan, I think one of the biggest obstacles is with data intelligence. It's sort of like being dropped off in the middle of the ocean, you know, which direction do you start to swim? There's so much stuff out there, and it can be inside your walls, sometimes it's hard to know where to start, and sometimes you start with the end in mind of this is what we are trying to prove or trying to figure out, you can draw conclusions from your data that represent what you're trying to achieve, right, so maybe that's not the best way to do it. I think just sitting down and making sense of what you have, where you focus, so you're not becoming overwhelmed, I think that's one of the bigger struggles that people face.

Matt, what about a small venture funded company that is in the middle of everything?

We're a prime example of Echovate, right. We have the vision, we have these ideas of what we believe we can accomplish, and we run into a couple things. Either we don't have a big enough data set yet to really do something and roll it out in a public way, or we don't have the talent and time of that talent to be able to devote to that.

You know, when you're in a start up or venture-backed start up, you may not be able to hire a bunch of statisticians or PhD's to spend a year or two years to figure things out. So, I think those are some issues. There's an interesting website out there called Kaggle, and it's basically crowd source predictive modeling and things like that, so there are all these things you can tap into as a smaller company, but I think usually it's about finding the talent, finding the data, and putting it together.

We have been fortunate enough where we have some smart PhD's that we've been working with, we have some folks that have been around the block when it comes to data and they have analyzed large, large sets and made sense of them, so I think we are fortunate in that regards, and any kind of smaller organization needs to think about how they are going to solve for that because that's not an easy to fill role, and obviously if you're reading any of the headlines, data scientists are in high demand.

Matt, I know one of the biggest issues I address via a question from every-body that I've talked to on the show: where they feel the skill gaps are going to be the most critical? I mean, when you are starting to get into the data game for your own organization, and you're trying to build into your decision making process, data you need to have high levels of reliability on, from a data scientist to an analyst, to somebody who can interpret the data and mash it up between external head of analysis to internal customer satisfaction, right? Trying to come up with outcomes and marry those up with whatever you are trying to get to mission-wise for your company, and so it's been pretty much across the board is you're just going to have to find smart people, and kind of go from there, and home grow a lot of it, because you can't just find that person. There are just not enough of them out there. Data scientist-wise.

Yeah Bryan, I would agree with that, too, and I would also say you can start small as well. Whether you are in a big organization or a small organization, you can say, let's look at this stuff and see if there are any trends, and start to go down that path. I've talked to and seen organizations where they want to have this sort of holy grail at the end of doing some sort of a data study, and you know, writing some code around it, whereas if you can test some assumptions and some theories and say ok, that's relatively interesting, we believe we could support that, now let's do sort of a bigger crunch on this, you know, that makes a lot of sense. I think as it relates back to talent, in the form of data scientists, it's easier to kind of get started and have those conversations, and of course, that's what we're doing, where you can scratch the surface a little bit, you can move it down the line, and then you can say ok, we are willing to take time and make the investment in really going down this path for a while and see what we can find.

Matt, that makes complete sense. So, how does social data, social sensing, social media information, how does that change things, or does it really make a difference from a data perspective on the human capital side of this equation?

I mean, it certainly does, Bryan, because this is information that a person is putting out, whether it's on Facebook, Twitter, Instagram, whatever it might be, all the time, and I think there are a lot of interesting information that you can discover around that. However, I've seen companies that they want to make sense of social media data, they want to make sense of Facebook data because it sounds sexy, where the reality is it might be total shit. And so while social sensing I think is something that's important, at least our approach is let's look at the data in a way that is not skewed by brands, and what's going to sound good in a headline or anything like that. But really, what are we trying to achieve and solve for, and what is the data that is going to get us there and sort of prove out what we hope to and what we think in a real way. You also have to be careful when you're looking at social data from a legal perspective, from a privacy perspective, and human capital management can have an adverse impact and things like that.

Absolutely. Matt, that's probably one of the things from a human capital, HR side of the world that we've both been involved with for a number of years is just at what point and how far can you push that information, who uses it, how risk averse, to the point of making yourself a little bit ignorant of information, do you have to be, right? It's a pretty typical business scenario where do you just not look, right? Like head in the sand-I didn't see it, I didn't hear it, you know, hands in your ears type thing.

Bryan, just to touch on that for a minute, it's interesting because, at least from our view of the world as we look at data and we look at data intelligence, we are trying to do something for our customer at the end of the day, and that's where our center of the universe is. That's what's important for us. And I think sometimes as it pertains to, it can be social, I think what's interesting around there is when you think about a candidate that applies to an organization, can you make that a frictionless process where they simply just press a button and apply via Linked In or Facebook. They don't have to answer any questions, they don't have to upload any resumes, and based on that, the machine learning data engine in the background is able to create a profile on that person that is meaningful that that manager can use in making educated decisions. I think that's where it gets really interesting.

You bring up a term that I haven't had a chance to jump in with anybody yet, Matt. Machine learning, where do people get started, just give them the nickel version of your take on where to get started in even getting their head around what that means and maybe how it can help them in their business.

You know Bryan, I think machine learning is for some businesses, and it's not for every businesses. Right? I think where it makes sense is where you can further explore, your algorithms, the construction of your data, can you learn in real time for that and become smarted based on these data inputs to build this model that helps further with predictions and decisions rather than just saying hey, here is something for a program, go out and put these updates in there. So, I think it's a really interesting space to explore, and I feel where you get started with that, you've got to find someone who understands that really well, and there's a lot of people that are software engineers, programmers, and they say oh yeah, I know about machine learning, but they really don't.

I think it's important that if you're going down that road and you're working with somebody, that you're working with somebody that understands the bigger context of machine learning. If nothing else, just from the very high level, 30,000 feet view, you actually need someone who can execute on it. But that's another—and it's interesting, machine learning and big data people say it's all-together; it's sort of all the same, and it's really not. It depends on how you're going to use it in your organization, and what it means, and how you, again, it goes back to talent, how do you get the people who can really do that in an intelligent way?

Matt, share some thoughts for those just getting started with data, and you've been focused on this for quite some time, kind of the data intelligence field, and what are some of the things that you can help people avoid some of those completely bullshit traps that you fall into, like avoid some of the mess. What are one or two tips you can give them in kind of looking at data and starting down this process?

You know Bryan, it's an interesting and almost sort of a difficult question, but I think it's really around focus. It's all around focus. I think that you can get overwhelmed with all the data that are out there. You can go to the Bureau of Labor Statistics and grab data. I mean, it's a mountain; it's a sea of data that's out there. So, I think that's a rat hole to go down that people can all the sudden you can say wait, we haven't made any progress here. So, again, just from our experience, we do—we have a specific focus on if you wonder if there's a correlation between this and this, and if so, how would we actually solve for that, and oftentimes, it starts with a very simple white board session. And then we start to look at that, and then we say, ok, laptops are closed at that point and we white board it out. If it makes sense, we say ok, what data do we need, do we believe, in order to make that happen? And then, do we have that data yes or no? If yes, great, then we get it, and if no, then where and how would we get that data? And then how much of it do we need?

Sometimes, again, human capital-based, you might need data that is 6 months, 9 months into it, right, to really get some sort of validity in that data, but I think to answer your question, I would just be hyper-focused, and figure out what's the one small thing you want to solve for, and then solve for that. In doing that, you're going to learn a shit ton about the process and you're going to learn about what works, what doesn't work, and then you can iterate and build from there.

Sure thing, Matt I feel focus is one of the things that I've heard come up because as you said, there's a lot of data available that you can run different ways and draw false conclusions that could detrimentally affect your business because you don't understand it.

Bryan, I agree with that, and I think within data, there's human psychology, right? So, I think this is relevant, but I was reading a magazine the other day and toward the back of the magazine, there's an ad for this weight loss pill, and they said people that took our pill lost 80% more compared to those who did not take our pill. And my first thought when I saw that is, is that because the pill actually works, or is it because the people that took the time to go out and buy that pill were willing to invest their hard-earned money, and so they are more committed to a weight loss program than their counterparts sitting next to them.

So, to me, that's also part of the big data conversation, or the data conversation, because that weight loss company, they can spin it however they want to spin it from a marketing perspective, but you know, we can challenge and ask questions around that and say is that really the reason or is there something else at hand that we really don't know about?

Well, and asking the better questions, right? That's the big point here—

Bryan yes, that's it, asking the better questions.

But people don't do it. So I think if you're going to do something right, make sure you don't have the same people sitting around the table all shaking their head going great, yay, all the yes culture, and have people pushing back saying uhh, I don't know, I mean, I think that tension, that creative tension on pulling that apart, is where things get a hell of a lot more effective. Sometimes it's a little bumpy. You've got to put your seatbelt on, but that's all right.

Well, I also think too, Bryan, this is something I preach internally at Echovate, is you have to be willing to call bullshit on your own data, right? And I've seen other, especially larger companies, where they are a little more reluctant to do that and to say, you know, listen, either what we are trying to solve for, no one cares about, or the manner in which we are trying to solve for—or the data that we are using is just not working, and so there's part of it—when we do this, who gives a shit if we can prove that or not, or we'll get into these debates back and forth—well, I can argue it this way based on the data, I can interpret the data this way, and you can interpret it this way, you know, there's a whole human element to this that people really need to be aware of when you are looking at data.

Great points Matt, I feel those are all things that I hope people really take to heart and think about because they are going to learn it sooner or later, I mean, that's the beauty of it. There are all iterations of this, and hopefully there's some value out of some of the tips you've given. You've been looking at this for quite some time.

Matt, I'll ask you to put on your futurism hat. 10 years from now, what does this conversation look like 10 years from now?

Bryan, the conversation won't even be around data, it'll just be—it's sort of like you look back, I'm going to date myself here for a second, but you look back and say hey, I'm going to stop at a pay phone and make a phone call, and then it was hey, I have a pager, and now I'm going to stop at a pay phone and call, that sort of thing. I think we're going to look back on this, it may seem sexy now, but it's just going to become the normalcy of how we do business and how we make decisions in the future. I think what's going to happen is right now we are in the research and development phase of the life cycle of data and data intelligence. I think that this stuff is just going to be commonplace in everything we do. I mean, you look at what IBM and Watson is doing. Obviously that's on a big scale, and obviously it's IBM, but why can't that layer of technology be on my new iPhone? That level of sort of transparency and the mark of, it's just going to be commonplace.

Matt, I feel a big driver of transparency, ultimately has been big data. It's been around quite some time. I think it really got going, at least I was exposed to it in the late 90s, and so we were able to start doing some things years ago, and so we are a long way past the mid 90s, and now it's about having the information giving you high reliability around decisions. That's the game, is having data get more intelligent.

Bryan, I think doing all that in an automated and frictionless way. I think it's a super exciting time, both in mature organizations, and also in start ups that we can harness these massive datasets that are publicly available out there, and you can leverage them within your own organization or your client's organization to really use this to do business in a way that we were never able to do 50 years ago, and I think that is just an amazing thing, it's an amazing step forward for business.

I really feel data access makes small businesses that much more competitive and large business that much more agile. To me, I think that's the two things that I hope companies think about because that's literally how I think about it. All of the many ways that the small business can just be lethal, as far as execution, now they've got better information, but also the big companies, if they can get that information harnessed, the agility starts to come into play again. Because they can move faster based on reliable information.

This relates 100% to talent because at the end of the day, you've got to be able to predict and get to the best talent you can and execute on whatever your business model is.

Bryan, that's right. I know we're almost at our time here, but the other element is, I consider it a huge win for the candidate because now, hopefully, they are being judged, right? And that's really what is happening. They are being judged and screened for a position in hopefully a much more objective, fact-based, data-driven way that is consistent across whatever platform a company might be using, and I think that's a real positive impact for that candidate across the board.

Jessica Miller-Merrell, Xceptional HR
HR Big Data Is Really Small Data

Welcome Jessica Miller-Merrell, workplace anthropologist and field analyst. Founder of blogging4jobs.com, HR blogger, Xceptional HR. She's an author and also a fellow show host for a podcast called Workology.

Jess, you've been focused on data for years—you have a personal data mindset, and you were a data-driven HR practitioner. Right off the bat—do you have any issues with the term big data?

Bryan, it's just kind of an ugly term, honestly. And It kind of is intimidating, especially if you are new to big data itself. It sounds just kind of scary, and I guess in a way it is. When I think of big data, it is pulling billions or trillions or infinity amount of information, maybe it's customer data or user information, different things like that, and when you use it in the context of human resources or the workplace, let's say that we are looking at applications or maybe things that you update or changes that you've made within your employees records, there are not trillions of updates or trillions of candidates contained within those two HR technologies, so in reality, big data in HR is not really big data. It is small data, and I think that's an important distinction mostly because we don't have to think about it in such large terms. The data that we likely have within our organizations, whether it's within our HRIS, our benefits information system, our scheduling system, applicant tracking system, whatever, we can pull and extrapolate that data and then begin to look for patterns and the analysis to help us make better decisions.

So, looking at small data, which I love the term we've had so far on the show, just a few episodes in, we've had people refer to it, Michael Harms referred to it as medium-sized data, and those I think are nice riffs on what it is. I mean, it's data, right? But data is pretty generic.

Jess, what are top priorities that you can start looking at, like workforce data, talent acquisition and management data, and start addressing without having to be a data scientist, in your opinion?

So I've spent a lot of time in this area because I'm not a data scientist, I'm an HR lady who has an interest in big data and is just kind of a geek, and I spent a lot of time in Silicon Valley, lived there for about 14 months before heading back to the Midwest, where this is now my home, I went to lots and lots of big data meetings and conferences and events, and there is literally in the bay area, in Northern California, there are probably 15 big data meet ups. So, it's a great way to absorb the information, and even honestly Stanford has three classes where you can go to talks, or different videos you can go online and learn and kind of get into the mind of these data scientists.

Bryan, when we think about big data, there are fundamentally the three V's. That's volume, velocity, and variety. So, you want to think about the data that you're pulling and the information contained within those V's. When we look at some data sources, there are really two different sources. There's internal, that could be your employee scheduler, or forecasting. Most of us, if you're in the retail market or some arena where people have to be at a certain place at a certain time have likely used. So, we are already utilizing big data or small data in order to make better predictive decisions in who shows up and when they show up to service customers and promotions and improving workforce productivity.

So once again going on the forecasting model. Existing applicant tracking system, you account communities, your internal social networks. It's interesting to think about if people are active on those social networks, they feel more engaged. If you can tie engagement to involuntary or voluntary termination, so what activity triggers disengagement in your workplace? Is it due to maybe not a lot of activity in the internal social network and hey they are also working maybe a crappy work schedule.

As far as external data, you can look at job seeker patterns, where are they going, what are they doing on the Internet and other activities. Competitor information, what are the competitors doing, when are they posting, what are they saying, what are their employees saying and then lastly social media. The one thing I want to mention about social, which I am definitely a fan of social media, I've written a book about how to use Twitter for business, but I am concerned about the activity particularly on the Internet and social media, whether it's Meetup.com, Twitter, or Facebook, wherever you are pulling this information from, that we are discriminating against those, the data of people who are not sharing. Those are important considerations to think about because there are many people who don't participate in the social space or are sharing their lives on social networks, and so we just need to be cognizant when we are pulling that data, that there are a number of folks, millions or billions even if you can believe, that aren't being active on social media. So, our data, our big data sources externally anyway, could be a little bit skewed or misrepresented.

Jess, great points and that's interesting that an ides or socialization that is being factored into or correlated probably more anecdotally than objectively is around engagement. If you're an engaged social media person, that you're going to be an employee who is engaged, and I think that's probably, I would like to see anybody provide data that could prove that because I absolutely don't believe that. What are your thoughts on that?

Bryan, I don't think it's because you're active on social media it means that you're engaged or disengaged. I mean, my view of engagement when it comes to the workplace is it's pretty fluid. I mean, I can go from being disengaged to engaged in a day or multiple times a day. There are times when I'm really productive, I'm engaged, I'm excited maybe about a project or I'm working with a team, or maybe we're just producing great results. That doesn't necessarily mean that I am going to be Tweeting or sharing. People react to different situations extremely uniquely. I will say for me, if I'm busy on a project or I am participating, I think many people are like this who are kind of master multitasksers, for scheduling those things. So, I might really hate my job, but I might be really active on social media because I am putting up appearances, and I think a number of smart marketers that are out there are thinking about those things. You need to be present on the Internet so that you can still be top of mind.

Jess, what are some measurements currently that are not being utilized within the workforce function that you feel that small to medium-sized data would actually help the talent function?

I would like to be able to see in terms of small data, the candidates within your ATS, maybe where they're located. Especially if you're building a talent community, you have those people within your applicant tracking system. Let's say these are heat maps together, and then quickly you're in a staff meeting and somebody says we're looking to open a call center in Salt Lake City, and you can immediately pull up from the data points that you've pulled to look up and see ok, what does my candidate pool look like, available candidates who have expressed interest maybe in the last 24 months that are in the Salt Lake City area. So, you can pull it up and determine, or at least discuss in some of the early stages, how much work are we going to have to do to be able to move forward in building a pipeline of candidates.

I'm definitely a fan of using this talent management data to align with your sales results and projections because think about this. I have had situations where in my practitioner HR career, someone has come into my office and said Jessica, we are adding 250 positions at XYZ call center, and we need to do it by mid-Q2. Well, mid-Q2 is just three weeks away, and if I know that I have to interview 7 people before I make one hire, that's a lot of people to be able to sort through and interview, and I just didn't have the bandwidth for it. So, if you're sitting down with your senior leaders, even if it's not me, somebody who is thinking about talent, maybe it's your CEO, they can build in while they are looking at sales projections and results and shifting business. In this particular, we were shifting about $25,000,000 from the field to one of the call centers, I needed to have a plan and we could put in projections so people could understand hey, my team can—this is the bandwidth we can handle. The solution is to maybe stagger the growth or bring in some contractors or plan in advance even, to start to build the pipeline to add to your organization.

The last thing that I'll say as far as ways that I see big data is succession planning. This is something that we're thinking more about. How are we using this information not just to engage our current employees, but retain them and help them grow. There were more people that left their job voluntarily in September 2014 that the sheer number in the US was more than the entire population of Oregon. So, it's important to think about these things. So, what happens if your people, there's a mass exodus in this current job seeker driven economy? Do you have the people in place to shift what's your game plan? Do we have these projections and plans and then pull in the data to help us make better decisions, and more informed decisions. Hopefully we can even anticipate maybe movement happening in our space so that we can get ahead of the game for a change.

Jess, do you feel phase I of working, like HR working more in depth with data is being more accurate in how you react, or being more proactive in how you get ahead of issues that are coming toward you?

I think it's both Bryan. So, typically HR has seen personnel as more of an administrative function, and there has been a lot of discussion in the HR space, particularly Harvard Business Review had a really great article about making the moves to separate the administrative and the strategic part of human resources. I personally think they can operate together in the same space. However, I think that we need to be proactive, and use the data to help us make those forward thinking decisions, but we should be using the data to continue to grow and change.

> *"Only a fraction of HR teams are taking advantage of all the information that we have out there to help them make smarter and more predictive and proactive decisions."*
>
> —Jessica Miller-Merrell.

Our senior leaders need this information, CEOs; talent is the number one top of my issue right now. HR for a long time is being seen as less strategy, more personnel and administrative based. When using big data and this information I already have available in our organizations, analyzing the patterns, we're able to come to our senior leaders and say hey, let me use this information that I have to help make better decisions so the business can go further and move more quickly. That is the best way to be able to build a strategic partnership within the business. You'll have lots of friends because you have all this data. One thing I wanted to mention is 49% of business leaders are agreeing that big data analysis and these results has helped improve decision-making in the human resource space, in general also.

They are looking at big data. However, only a fraction of HR teams are taking advantage of all the information that we have out there to help them make smarter and more predictive and proactive decisions. Now this stat is from a Deloitte survey. I am definitely of the mind that big data can help us be proactive and more strategic in our decision-making. You just have to make a decision as an HR practitioner, what's the most important thing for your business? Are you going to be chasing tail and being reactive or do we need to be looking proactive, and do you have the staff and the time and the budget to make that happen. Or, can you afford not to take advantage of all the information and data that you have at your fingertips?

Jessica, do you feel that one of the things that we're going to run into are the issues that I feel the workforce analytics is going to run into is it's going to be stirring the same pot? It's going to be looking at the same information because we've all had, I mean, everybody that has been in the HR space or the talent function space has had kind of the same information for a long time, it just depends on what package you run it through software-wise, or what different potential report you look at it. So, is it now marrying it up with different parts of the business information, or external data that you can now start to draw some different conclusions or correlations with the information?

Absolutely Bryan. Big data, this predictive data, this intelligent data that we are pulling from and using to make our decisions is not simply a dashboard. It's not that dashboard that you log in when you go into your applicant tracking system or your HR tech suite. That dashboard that tells you what your turnover is, how many opening up requisitions you have, the number of candidates for this opening that you're interviewing for, or maybe what performance level you're recruiting team is, how are they taking care, what is the time to hire, all of those things. Big data is much more complicated than that. It's not just something that we can look at on a spreadsheet or put in our little Excel formulas and say, hey, my recruiters are making 50 calls a day, they are doing XYZ, and they are filling positions 15 days faster than Q1. That's not big data. Big data looks at many different things, things that you wouldn't necessarily consider a factor. It could be external information, maybe you're looking at patterns in terms of reduction of force, where people are moving throughout the US, demographic information, unemployment, these are things that could be helping you make the decision to, oh, if I know that unemployment is low in this particular area, we need to maybe make some tweaks and changes to our existing recruiting strategy, especially if it is important that we fill these positions quickly.

One example of that is pretty well known in the space when it comes to one of the first business cases for HR in big data is Xerox. So, Xerox actually eliminated the traditional job interview and their call centers. And for those of us who are in HR, that is kind of crazy. Think about it. I know I've worked in the call center, I've been the head of HR, and you do all these interviews, the manager interviews, and no conversation with the candidates. So, there were no more traditional job interviews.

They relied simply on assessments and tasks to determine whether or not this person was qualified to do the job. And what they found in looking at the analysis and understanding people and what really the break even analysis of how long did this person need to stick around after we spent money in recruiting and training and then understanding what the expected results were, they determined that really, that person only needed to be in that organization for 10 months and then after if they left, then they had made their money. So, this hiring process using the data, allowed them to reduce their turnover dramatically. So, it's sort of eliminating the human but factor a little bit and relying solely on data, and it also took out the lost productivity by managers and hiring managers and recruiters who were starting and stopping and running to those interview rooms or picking up the phones to qualify candidates and facilitate those interviews.

Don't just think about your dashboard or the traditional sense of things. Sometimes, big data leads you to a place, like completely eliminating interviews, and that's maybe something that you have to reconsider. It's also extremely scary. I mean, think about it, no interviews. How do I know this person is going to work with Jimmy John, my regional rep for the call center? That's the risk that the data is telling you it's worth taking.

Jess, a two part question—what percentage do you feel that this, the screening selection, hiring process, can be automated using data intelligence, first half of the question. And second question, do you foresee the future as taking out the subjectivity literally as much as possible? Taking the people out of the equation in the hiring process?

So, I'm definitely a fan of humans Bryan, and the human element of things. However, I do believe in situations where you are kind of ever-green hiring, using data intelligence can really help you maximize your dollars spent, your productivity, and your time. And things like retail, call center, places where we are hiring lots and lots of people, secretaries even, depending upon maybe data entry, these sorts of things we can test for. And I don't necessarily think that the human element needs to be present. This is going to cause a lot of push back, maybe in your organization, or maybe it's giving you the shakes a little bit. I know it would for me because I do like to get to know somebody before I bring them on board or know that I am going to be able to work with them; however, when you are looking at sheer volume or the bigger picture, and you have 10 of these call centers that are like this, I mean, imagine the productivity and the time spent. These small instances of discomfort or potential employee relations issues, that risk is not outweighed. So, the productivity and the cost savings, and the success rate, it speaks for itself.

I think the main thing, if you're thinking about starting something like this is what I call a lighthouse, and it's a term that my friend Stacie Chapman has turned me on to. I used to call them pilot programs, and pilot just kind of has this negative connotation, but lighthouse it's like wow, this is a possibility. So, a lighthouse is just a small task. Let's try a new program for 30, 60, 90 days. And let's see what the results are. And we did this with assessments in my last job where we actually created and implemented a sales assessment, and completely redid the entire hiring process for one of my call centers, and it was interesting because there was no assessment prior to this, and we went through a pretty sort of scientific process to sit down and try to understand what our top performers were doing. And we went through the first phase of the new assessment process. We tested everybody in our call center, and this is a small sample size because we didn't have tons of people, but we brought them in, they took the test, and based on their results, we looked at where they were in terms of meeting their goals and expectations for sales. And then determined this sweet spot for hiring, for people who had this score were going to be X successful in this particular role.

So, 8 months into testing this, I realized that we had a glitch in the system, and we had been hiring people who weren't passing assessment. Which, at first was kind of scary, but when you look back at it, it was actually a good thing because it was able to prove the hypothesis and all this work that we put into play because 85-95% of people who would not have passed the assessment, they did not last 30 days. So, it helped me prove the hypothesis, and allowed us to expand the assessment not just in our sales call center, but also to different parts and divisions of the organization.

Thank you for sharing that quasi-case study Jess and the kind-of-how you implemented with the bonus of the outcomes, solid stuff here. What field is the biggest threat for this entire new data frontier getting inserted into the HR processes?

It's happening. This is the reality. And why wouldn't we want to have more information to make better decisions, or the right information instead of following our guts or just kind of operating under this constant state of reactivity where we are going from fire to fire. Using big data helps us to predict so that when we are juggling all these balls in the air, think about talent management, we are juggling 7 or 8 balls at one time, we are trying to do our best, and then suddenly there is a fire and a focus on one of those balls, so we move our attention to that single ball. The others kind of fall, right? We lose focus, they fall, and then what ends up happening is because we haven't been giving the rest of those balls we have been juggling attention, the fire moves or the focus moves to the next. Big data helps you juggle those balls and being able to move throughout all 6 or 7 balls at a time, whatever the number is, whatever your focuses are within the organization, and anticipate so that you can make good decisions instead of working in this reactive, freak out mode. I know that big data, and I will tell you there are companies that are employing and hiring big data scientists just to focus in the human capital space.

It's not if this is coming, it is coming. For many companies, it is already here.

I just think the important thing for us to understand is HR folks; we don't have to be the big data scientists with all the answers, and the real key is to work with baby steps. So, start small, you don't have to be a rock star, but take on small steps, come up with little wins, and then you can kind of build your business case from that.

Jess, are there any resources that you could point some folks to or that you hold near and dear that will help with this data intelligence learning curve for folks?

Aberdeen has some nice workforce analytics white paper: Workforce analytics in retail. There's another really nice article from Forbes, it's called: Meet the New Boss of Big Data, and that explains the Xerox case study. They also have a nice webinar that's available on demand if you just go to the webinar, the learning management section, you can download that. I have a research document, or kind of a white paper, that I titled, what's the Big Deal About Big Data? That will be coming out in Q2 and focusing on big data for human resources and kind of giving you the basics with some nice case studies so that we can kind of take it from a HR, human capital point of view instead of what we're seeing a lot of is the data scientists kind of driving the conversation, and I'm happy that they are driving the conversation, however they are really focused on what they do best and not really putting themselves in our shoes.

I've heard them talk about meetings, and it always cracks me up a little bit. They do address the fact that not everybody thinks like them, not everybody is a data scientist, so they talk a lot about how to put data and information that they are collecting and the patterns that they see into layman's terms. And so that's why you see a lot of these data visualizations polls, and infographics and heat maps because it's a way for those of us who are not data scientists and trained in the profession to understand and help sort of really focus on what the data means to drive these decisions.

Jess, I love the fact that we are going to make the workforce analytics and the HR function much more objective so we can start hopefully socialize that data as people start getting datasets and get it into where we can start seeing it in a more transparent way. Laser-in on how good or how poor a candidate experience is within a organizations recruiting process.

Matt Charney, Recruiting Daily

Back to the Future

Welcome Matt Charney, Executive editor and head of content from Recruiting Daily. Welcome to Thug Metrics Matt.

Yes. What up Bryan?

Hey, I've been waiting to have you on the show so we can we can get a little thug, right? That's what it's all about. That's what I was hoping to do, you know. Always got to keep it gangsta, as it were.

Yes, you're still the same little G, but you keep it low key, which is what I really appreciate.

Well Matt, let's see what you know, I really would like to get as many of your thoughts, you talk with a lot of people, being from the media space and creating content, doing a lot of writing, and you do a lot of research. But first of all, tell us a little bit about who you work for, what you do, and then I've got the first question queued up right here.

Essentially what I do, I manage all of the content and editorial strategy for Recruiting Daily, which is a portfolio of websites, recruitingdaily. com, or recrutingblog.com are probably the most pertinent. But essentially what we cover is content created by recruiters for recruiters. We are the largest content destination in the world, and the first as well, that is dedicated specifically to recruiting talent acquisitions. So, a lot of that involves talking to the vendors, talking to our members, and really staying in touch with what's going on in the industry so we can deliver content information that's actually going to help them do their job more affectively.

Matt, what is the current trend toward big data in recruiting in talent acquisition?

Yes. Bryan I think that it is at that point where it's a very amorphous buzzword. It's very front-of-mind, certainly. I think big data is up there with social recruiting, mobile recruiting, and candidate experience right now with kind of those ubiquitous talking terms. But I think at the same time where it's sort of at is that while people are talking about it, and they know it's really important, and they know that it's an essential kind of medium and discipline to bring to the recruiting process, at the same time I think that the average recruiter is really scared about big data because of the fact that, a) it holds them a little bit more accountable, which is something that has not necessarily happened in the past, but I also think that it being a bastion of liberal arts majors, and those who have fallen into the profession without a lot of barriers of entry, what you have is a general sphere of anything that reeks of math.

So, because it is in the best interest to work with them predicated on gut feeling, and judgment I think that what you're really seeing is a knowledge and understanding that you have to be adding the objective to the process, but at the same time still placing a high premium on sort of the more subjective stuff like the gut feelings that go into determining whether or not a candidate's going to move through the process. I think that recruiters largely are concerned with getting jobs filled as quickly as possible. So, they generally tend to be more shortsighted, I think. So, when it comes to a buy-in like, let's say, predictive analytics to even who creates future advocacy, taking the time to lay that ground work is really secondary to getting at them now. I think that's largely something that recruiters can do without applying any sort of data, but yes the fear then comes in; is this actually going to make me more efficient because it's going to, at best, be at opposing odds with my current metrics which is how I get the positions filled.

Matt, I definitely understand and get where people come from, that it's the reactionary, because I think recruiting, unfortunately, is a reactionary type role, because you're kind of at the end of the tail, and so you get wagged constantly, and you're always responding everything that everybody says, so it's very hard unless you're a different type of talent acquisition or recruiting structure than from what I've seen is, to be more of a; you're out there building a client base of passive candidates that you're building relationships with, that's one side, or you're out there just trying to track down all the conversations possible and then cue up, get narrowed down to two or three, get those in front if your hiring managers, and if it works it works, get an offer pulled through, and then you roll on to the next one, right? So, it's one of the two. You're either building relationships or a kind of book of candidates, or you're out there just slamming, you know, talent through the system to try and get open jobs filled, right? Am I missing—any other things you would consider part of recruiting?

No. I do think, certainly the building of relationships is tantamount to both Bryan. At some point you have a focus on building relationships with candidates and the other, you know, the distance/time side it's more building that relationship with clients because hopefully one will have fed the other. But yes, I certainly do think that most of recruiting, to your point, is predicated on the demand of people who are not used to any of your clients and your candidates, and between them there's so much variability in terms of things like timing and outcomes. It becomes really interesting because there's no structure standardized process really, in order to get things done, other than, you know, people trying to get it done. So, it's basically a hustle at this point in time.

Got it Matt. So, what parts of, and this is a conversation I truly do enjoy having being from the recruiting side of the house, you know, years ago, doing that for several years, total appreciation for the hard work that goes into it and also total appreciation for the complete laziness that happens depending on what type of recruiter you are or what type of culture you're in. I've seen it both. Where can data intelligence be applied in the process? Where can you take the person out of it and put the robot in to run the data?

Bryan. Yes. I think that's a really good question and I certainly thing that right now there's a huge gap in both capability and technology to do a lot of that. For instance, right now, you have a staff that I would consider fundamental for sourcing and recruiting advocacy that is the source of hire. That is something that is eminently measurable; where are my candidates coming from and where is my time best spent? In a recent poll actually, I think it was CareerBuilder that did it, that 25% of recruiters, and these are ones who actually admitted it, said that they had no way of tracking source of hire, and a huge majority of the companies that actually record it by the candidate or manually enter it by the recruiter. What you have from the recruiter side of, let's say that I found a candidate on Monster for instance, and then I'm going to enter it as direct source so I sound cool because I'm uploading it. On the candidate side that often tends to either be the first, or what they think is going to be the best answer to that question.

So, it's a really imprecise science. On top of that what you're getting are things like, most candidates start their job search right now by going to Google, they'll type in something like engineering jobs in San Jose. From there the first results are going to be Indeed, and then Indeeds' first results are going to be, let's say, Glass Storage as opposed to Glassdoor. What exactly is the source of hire there becomes a really interesting question and right now, unfortunately, there's no real way to measure that in most systems. And I think that that certainly extends then to a lot of elements of the recruiting process because of the fact that every stage is more or less to strengthen. So, when you have quality of hire, which is not in any way, tracked back to an applicant tracking system because of the fact of things like, employee performance and employee productivity will live in a completely different world. So, I think where a lot of the automation has to begin becomes picking and tying the parts of the process together and really laying the framework for measurement that's important, but also being able to track it, not only throughout the recruiting process, which doesn't exist, but also being able to track it through the entire employee lifecycle process from hire to retire, as they say.

Matt, where do you see the high touch side of recruiting really working the best? I came from the days of, you know, we used to source candidates, right, and then skill market them into organizations, and build relationships with the candidate and the hiring manager side, right? That's totally old school almost pre-internet, not quite, but pre-internet, pre-social. And so, the high touch side of it, where—I know we're going more to the recruiting side, but this is a lot of what you're world is, where do you see an industry that high touch has to happen with candidates? You can't really automate a lot of it because it just, the candidates—the talent pool is not right for it.

Well, Bryan I think that you can obviously automate a lot more when it comes to high volume, high turnover positions, so things like hospitality, restaurant industry, call center, customer service, that sort of thing, because of the fact that there are very easy to adjudicate assessments and baseline for; is somebody going to be able to do this job. Where I think high touch comes in is actually in industries knowledge and it's more, I would say that's it's a positive correlation between the amount of skill set that a job entails and the amount of high touch that's required. I certainly think that the big shift that is happening has happened as a result of automation and that is that you have things like profile aggregators, or social networks, or even the kind of middle-ware tools that have dynamic profiling within an applicant tracking system. What this has meant is that people's information is now is easily defined.

Back in the day you'd have to call into a company directory, you'd have to rely on professional association trade journal, you really had to get clever about finding people's information, but it's really become less of a commodity; as a result of that, because I'm able to see the same information as everyone else. Ninety two percent, I think, right now of Fortune 500 companies are customers of LinkedIn and Enterprise, which means that being probably the first place they go, they're seeing the same results as everything else.

Where I think high touch comes in is not finding the candidates which used to be the premium place of recruiting, but being able to get them on the phone, or being able to get them to respond to an email, or any other call to action. That's really where that high touch element comes in. But once that dialogue is established certainly I think that a lot of automation can and is happening when it comes to things like Talent Network, a targeted email list, and other things, once that candidate migrates into the data base.

Do you see big data drastically affecting how organizations approach their workforce branding Matt?

Yes. Bryan, I think that what you're seeing, obviously, and this is another one of those cliché topics. I'm going to go down and push reality here on my end. The shift is really is that recruiting is moving more towards the marketing discipline. With that it carries an obvious different set of analytics. You're looking at, say, being able to track things that are strictly online based, things like, Impression, and Flip Through, Upstream, and Downstream, user behavior conversions, cost per conversion, cost per hire, and that sort of thing. So I think by applying the marketing disciplines, through it, yes, you're going to see more of an emphasis on a player branding, but I think that that's going to largely drive more targeted online recruitment marketing and lots of an emphasis on creating a holistic ad based brand. I think you're going to get much more users based targeting and much less, what we stand for, who we are, and value statements, little flashing careers websites, as a result.

Matt, do you feel that more data's going to actually make the recruiting profession more agile or actually slow them down? Or nothing? Totally make or not make a difference?

Yes, so I think—Bryan, I think the data is probably not going to make a huge impact on speed, but what I do think it's going to make an impact on is quality. Right now if I have hundreds, and hundreds, and hundreds of resumes sitting in my data base for a single job, you know right now it's slowed down, but they're still getting an 85 to 200 applications on average for any posted positions depending on what study you read. I think that rather than it just kind of sitting in a data base and a recruiter going through that by being able to apply some algorithms and streaming tools on the front end, being able to rank more candidates automatically, and things of that nature, you're going to have that, you know, a recruiter being able to emphasize, really, on the top of the funnel, right? So, I feel the better candidates are going to naturally rise to surface and not get ignored, but at the same time to what we were talking about earlier, the fact that a hiring manager not getting macro feedback, or a candidate needing to push out an interview a week because they have a previous work commitment, I think things like that are always going to more or less make that speed element even out. But I think that speed will be impacted when it comes to identifying candidates faster, absolutely.

Okay. Well, that's definitely a good thing. Matt, do you think it's currently talent or technology that is going to slow down the adoption of data intelligence in recruiting function?

Bryan, I feel right now technology is absolutely the thing that's going to be slowing it down. If you look at applicant tracking systems with as much automation efficiencies you'd like to create, things are basically like—if you're looking at consumer technology you're playing an Xbox One and all of a sudden you're going back to a Commodore 64, right [laughter]? When it comes to moving through this stuff. So, I just think the limitations of technologies and the amount of money that companies have spent—so for instance right now, 85% of companies have no way for a candidate to apply or express interest in a job via mobile device. Another 70% won't even have their career site displayed on mobile because they're driven by these ancient applicant tracking systems that were built well before that was even a consideration.

And so I think that those kind of limitations in catching up to the market are obviously going to be highly impacting data because while you could be theoretically be collecting all these rich streams of data and using these to make better decisions at the same time, the limitations of the systems means that there's no way to either collect, interpret, or analyze that data because good luck pulling it out.

So, I guess if you are—well let me go a different direction. Is this really more applicable to company size, bigger companies, got all the resources, they're going to be the ones to be able to do it, so it's a big company conversation verses the majority of the market place?

Yes. Bryan, I definitely think that for companies that are doing relatively limited hires what you see as a general trend are things like referrals or internal mobility for openings that are much higher than at the other, like enterprise employers, multi-nationals, generally tend to rely much more on external candidates, third party recruiters, or POs and that sort of thing. I think that given that distinction and just being able to have the amount of data that determines hiring patterns, if you fill two positions a year, who cares about where they came from and what patterns you can analyze [laughter] and if your something that's doing 20,000 of them a year, than obviously you're collecting much more information points and are going to be able to watch for all these principal correlations, and also be able to apply it to a problem, whatever that may be.

Take note, Matt is a graduate of the USC Film School. Did I get that right?

Yes you did. It's the one school that Steven Spielberg couldn't get in. Bryan, that's true. He was rejected four times.

Matt, if you had a movie you could lay over the top of recruiting's struggle with big data, what would it be? I want to be open minded about this, the struggle or opportunity, what movie would that be?

Bryan, that's a darn good question. I think that it's really—I go all the way back to Back to the Future for the reason that right now we're living in 1985, but someone or some technology is really going to have hit 80 miles an hour and go back to1952 because that's where recruiting is compared to the rest of the world.

Nice. I think we just came up with a new segment for every show that we do on Thug Metrics. You've got to answer the movie question. That's a good answer.

I like it. No, I hope that worked [laughs].

Yes. We'll see how that goes for sure. Yes, and I agree. We're still very much stuck in—recruiting is such an interesting part of the overall talent function, the HR function, personnel function, whatever you want to call it. Because it is still handed off to—literally it's almost as like a sales function, right? Let's try you out in sales, and let's try you out in—and if that doesn't work we'll try you out in recruiting, right, because you're not tied to revenue as much, so we don't have to fire you. So it's an odd, interesting, in a place that people get tried out a lot, which is completely counter-intuitive, that that's who you want out representing your brand and working with all your hiring managers, if that's how it works. What's going to change recruiting in the next ten years?

I think the thing that's really going to change, Bryan, the most is exactly some of the stuff you're talking about. I think that it is going to become a more data driven discipline in the sense that I think that as systems increasingly integrate, what you're going to see is that the functions that are actually seen from the information that right now is limited to HR, are really going to be able to take away a lot of the decision making process from recruiting and really tie that back into larger business initiatives. I think on the one hand from a quanta-data perspective and overall what are our talent acquisitions goals and strategies, I think you're going to see that being tied back, a lot more into the business. I also think in correlation to that you're going to see a lot less people who are just coming into the profession, and you're going to see a lot more, I think, barriers to entry because as it becomes more of a business function, and human capital obviously becomes more critical as we're facing talent shortages across the board, and definitely an increased competition for skilled candidates. What I think you'll see is this becoming a much more specialized business function that requires a lot more training and barriers for entry than you're currently seeing, it's a free for all, so that they can support the business needs that are now measurable as opposed to, "Hey, whatever anyone can hire somebody for a job." I think we're going to start seeing a lot more confidence in this defined and standard analytics.

Good information Mr. Charney. Up next, cool or fool? Tell us something you think in the next year people is doing that's cool and something that you shouldn't do because it's fool.

One thing Bryan that I think that is cool right now is that you're starting to have recruiters actually focused on content marketing. People are actually learning how to write things like emailing authentications, job descriptions, which that was really basic. Unless you've ever read anything bad that's ever been posted on a career site or received an mail from a recruiter. I think that emphasis across the board is really cool. What I think it's cool is that people are still talking about mobile recruiting all over the place because right now obviously that shouldn't be an independent category because mobile is, and it's not a separately cracked conversation at all, nor should it be.

I think that the same thing extends to things like emerging markets. As you have companies that are moving much more to an offshore and outsource model, these people who obviously, if you look at internet and mobile adoption rate, since they're so tied together, so you're missing out on that, and you're missing out on that whole gen-Y millennial; why can't we hire them, But look how we're accessing content information, not to mention things like the software developers, engineers, or even casual job seekers. I mean internet usage now is mobile, so if you have an online process at all, you're just an idiot for not being on there, in my personal opinion, but at the same time yes, it is creating bias, but it's a more—but it's—who cares about the bias, you're just cheating yourself out of good candidates across the board, and more diversity than there ever was.

Steve Burton, Glassdoor

Use It or Lose It: Listen to Feedback

Welcome to Steve Burton.

I'm excited because you bring a different bag—a lot of data. I'm a big fan of your organization, Glassdoor. Steve is the VP of B to B marketing for Glassdoor, one of my favorite organizations because it's data centric and all about the conversation and a lot of data backing it. That makes for an interesting perspective. To kick it off, if you could just tell the listeners a little about yourself and then we'll jump right into it.

Yes. Bryan, my background has been tech for the last ten years, in various companies being, development, product management, and then marketing. I've worked at companies like Symantec, so, my whole background is really data and technical, and engineering. I recently, about a year ago joined Glassdoor, to do marketing in the B2B arch. It's been an exciting time and been a big transition for me, moving from a technical audience to a less cynical audience, but it's been hugely exciting, and as we get into the details, like you said, it's all about data. The big trend right now is big data, that's what everyone's trying to understand and figure out. We've got lots of opportunities from players who are looking to get into that space.

Steve, how does Glassdoor fit into the big data conversation?

Bryan, it's an easy place to start. Every seven seconds a new piece of data arrives at Glassdoor, which is based on an employer. First and foremost our data velocity is pretty significant and that's around six and a half million reviews on employers. So, every—almost every—every single second of every single day we're collecting big data about employers out there and we want to try to help those employers understand what that data translates to in terms of their employee brand, their employee sentiment, and what's really going on in their organization, and how they can improve.

Steve, how does—I mean, crowd sourcing, five or six years ago was, other than restaurants, was a fairly still new area of HR talent employment, branding, anything. How has that changed? How has that completely changed the game for, maybe the recruiting side, and also the candidate side?

Yes. I think first and foremost Bryan a lot more information is available today than it's ever been and that information is split across hundreds of different channels. You always have social media, you have Twitter, you have Facebook, you have LinkedIn, you've got Glassdoor Community, and you've got lots of online advertising channels, Job Box, Search Engines, as well as the traditional print. Since then the how of job seekers getting insight into jobs, or find jobs, or even understand employers, and really get a deep insight to whether they want to work at a company. It's completely changed. What that means to the employer is they've got to understand every one of those channels because that's their employer brand. It's what people, how people and job seekers perceive their brand in different locations. When you're on Facebook looking at the company page, are people talking about the employer on Facebook, in a discussion? Employers need to be there, then they can understand how their brand is being perceived, and they need to act on the information. In the first place you put a staff entering, measuring each of those channels, and then understanding how effective they are, how much of your candidates come through those channels. So, in terms of crowd-sourcing it's a huge opportunity for employers to get a competitive edge on their competitors in the look for talent, ultimately.

Bryan, what's scary is that most employers actually ban social media internally. I've looked at huge companies. They don't like you on Face-book. They don't like you on Twitter, or even LinkedIn because they feel it hampers their productivity. So, it's just the whole embracing of the channels, the new technology, and the new web working, shall we say, and there's a huge opportunity for employees to get on board and really use big data metrics across those channels to drive a competitive edge.

You bring up a classic great point Steve. It's a new generation or an uptake of command and control with the way that I think about it when you ban— when you ban social media, or you're trying to lock down the conversation and attribute it to better productivity, to me that's completely ass-back-wards to trying to be in better conversation with your customers, internal and external customers. Where, I mean, is there data that supports the companies that do that, have a worse, like their overall brand is much more on the negative side than the positive side?

Yes. I mean we've done some internal research at Glassdoor and we should have some specifics to publish it here in the next few weeks. But ultimately if you're an employer and you're doing employment branding, and you're doing that across social media channels, than you're really putting your story out there and influencing your brand, as opposed to standing back and just kind of watching it go by. Job seekers are actu-ally more willing to come and want to work for a company because they have a better understanding, they differentiate it, and ultimately you're engaged as an employer. You're not just letting people talk about your brand in the opportunity, you're part of the conversation. Definitely the correlation from employers that are doing branding which are ones that are, perhaps, ignoring the social media bandwagon and getting in it.

As I look at marketing for example, marketing five years ago it was largely about being creative, about having a nice website, nice banners, going to events, and really to differentiate it with marketing today, its analytics and metrics, and really understanding the customer, what they like and what they don't like. I see the opportunities from employers, and HR, and recruitment, to do the same about their candidates, so they really get an insight to what attracts candidates, and what detracts candidates, and which channels that can best influence them, so they can ultimately find the best people for their company.

Steve, it sounds like that you're saying HR should be more like marketing, which you're not the first person to say that, and hopefully not the last, but is that the direction that the best places to work, the brand leaders have all moved already, or are they still moving in that direction?

I think they're still moving in that direction Bryan. I feel what makes it the leaders and the best places to work is just they're embracing transparency, they're not fearing it, and then they're making it out of their ever day situation with how they manage culture, how they manage people, how they onboard people, and even how they interview prospects where, it's like "Hey we want to hear from you, can you please submit feedback"? It's like we want to come to you and continuously improve. So, I think the metrics come later, but the first step is really embracing the fact that information in your brand is everywhere and you need to be part of that conversation. If I look back at what why marketing got into metrics it was very similar to engineering. When I was in engineering we obviously had think tanks, we had reproduce issues, duplicate issues, and we let them die in engineering by metrics. You might have heard of agile methodology. I think marketing kind of took it, at least, out of that book.

Bryan, I really see the same for human resources. To give an example, if I said to you, when was the last time you could read pages of data, how many people in human resources, or in recruiting can say, in the last week, or in the last month? Or how many people visit the career page page, and how long did they spend on the career page? And I think this is where the opportunity is, to hedge our leaders. Once they can understand the effectiveness of their employer brand, and have it tell their story, they can improve it, they can understand what's working and what isn't working, and as soon as they get into that mindset as constantly evolving in the company so that just candidates know exactly what's going on, like today, or yesterday, that gives them a much more competitive landscape in how to beat their competition.

Steve, do you, and I know you just referenced this, do you feel that your software background has actually helped you as a marketer in marketing?

It's made me aware of the technology and trends Bryan, and how to embrace those and make them work in business. But you have to be careful. The audience in a technical world and an engineering background is very different to the recreating landscape. I see the opportunities clearly and it's huge. I mean, anyone who gets used to looking at Google analytics for example on the recruiting pages of their employer brands or look at social media metrics, and engagement in click-through, like that's really where you're going to see companies win and lose on how they can attract talent, because all of those candidates are out there on social media being very active in their stars and their feedback, and you've got to adapt, and you've got to use that really as the phase of the market.

Steve, I would definitely agree with you that from engineering, or software to recruiting is kind of like apples to air-conditioners [laughter]. Not really. It doesn't sync-up. But the beauty is the intersection is really cool because it is amazing, because you're managing all—recruiting is really about where people are at, where they're coming from, what they want, marrying that up with the same thing as far as what the job rate is, and what the company is, right? It's not overly complicated, but the human factor in it is where it gets more complicated. The best of the best are the ones that really understand the needs on both sides, both stakeholder groups, and how to get there with the least amount of friction.

So, that's where I think the analytics tend to be, you know, you should be able to manage that talent funnel, or the talent process in such a more kind of laser focused, kind of pinpoint effort. You don't really have to guess where things came from. There we go. Solved it all.

[Laughs] We all live happily ever after.

So, I've got to get—elephant in the room, Steve. What football club do you follow?

I follow Liverpool. Liverpool's my ball club.

Steve, what have been some surprises since you dug into the data, you've been there a little over a year, what part of the data has surprised you if any?

Yes. Bryan lots. When you look through the blogs, how employers are reacting to what's being spoken and told about every day, I think the first data that surprised me was the impact of acknowledging the information and acting on it. A good example of that is, if a review comes in for an employer, and the employer doesn't necessarily like the review, his first instinct is, "Hey, can you remove the review?" Actually it's in the employer's best interest to actually respond to a review. Most job seekers actually pause when they see the backstabbing plays and respond to the review. To most job seekers, actually when they see the fact that the employer is engaged in responding to reviews, the credibility, the authenticity of that action alone makes the jobseeker feel good about the company because they're part of the conversation. So I guess like, acting is better. It's tangible. It's real. We've had CEOs respond to employee reviews and as a result 35 job seekers who saw that action actually went back to the CEO and said, "Hey look, when I was researching the company, part of my decision was based on the fact that you were the only CEO that was responding to reviews.," and that says a lot about the company." So, I guess the first thing is just acknowledging and embracing, and acting really does work.

Number two is really, it's changing who you are, and again, if you look at the data—so for example when you—we give away this thing called Free Employer Account and it allows any employer to look into Glassdoor and see the metrics about the candidates who are researching them. We give them you full demographics of the users that are actually researching your profile. For example, how many male or female, what age of the people that are coming to the site, what's their backgrounds, what are the companies those people traditionally research after, their user profile, and for a lot of companies who have an employer brand, they have their own perception about what it really is, and what it means to them, and how special they, how unique. But the bottom line is if that brand isn't translating to jobseekers that want to apply and work at that company, then there's something wrong. So, think just looking at the level of insight you get on who's researching you, what jobs they're clicking on, and what attracts them, that allows the employers to change their brand, also personalize the brand to the right audience. And again, an opportunity can become more relevant. If a software engineer goes and visits the corporate group page and it's very corporate and very generic, it's not very exciting for the software engineer to learn about what it's like to be an engineer in that company. Whereas if you could personalize the corporate group page so that you knew it was software engineer, you could then make the content and everything more relevant.

It's looking at what is working, what isn't working, and then figuring out, how do we improve that? I think that certain levels of information, it's very compelling. I came from a tech company that was really successful and I looked at the reviews, I looked at the employee sentiment, and one thing that were common, there are no life/work bounds. Yet a lot of jobseekers go into a job search thinking, life/work bounds is important to me, but a lot of the top leading companies, that's a hard place to have a work/life bounds because everyone's working flat out, they're trying to beat the competition, they're trying to be more competitive. So, I think understanding why people are working in a company, and maybe why many people aren't, and then really acting on the information that you can see.

So, Steve, 61%, you had recently, Glassdoor recently published some research that said 61% of employees say that new job realities differ from expectations set during the interview process. How does big data actually make this better?

Big data gives the job seeker an accurate view in a matter of seconds. You can take all the information and you can present it to the right person, in the right format, and they can clearly understand that information, then they can make a decision immediately. Again, six and a half million reviews we can make it really easy for a job seeker or an employer who understands what it's like to really work at a company, and again, you can do it on your cell phone. You can download the app, but when you're on a bus or a train it might take 10, 15 seconds, you can read from real people about what it's really like to work there. I didn't have that when I got into engineering. I came out of college. A company promised me the full world, "Hey, you'll be working on these really cool projects, you'll be developing, and life will be good." and then when I started I was put on technical support. I spent a year fixing issues and I wanted to leave. I think that's the example. I didn't have something like Glassdoor that would have told me what the experience of engineers that recently joined. I think that's the power of big data. We can make better decisions quickly, and everyone's life improves as a result of it.

Big question coming at you Steve; has anybody ever asked you the question, how did you, or did you check out Glassdoor when you went to Glassdoor, in your interview process?

Yes [laughs]. And it was, I mean it looked too good to be true and it was my first experience in that and I did some digging. I looked through reviews that we're good and just like we do when we look at hotels, and we look to purchase anything, we want to see the best of both worlds.

Bryan, and again, seeing that that the CEOs responded, or the VP of sales has responded, it give you that, okay, things aren't perfect, but when they're not perfect, someone's actually listening. Someone actually care. So, yes—

I'm encouraged about that. You gave me an uptake on humanity right there that you actually used your own tool before you went to work for the organization.

Steve, do you have some predictions for the next five years?

Yes. I think, well firstly every company needs a data science group. Bryan, we're looking at having one at Glassdoor, and the level of insight we get, and the decisions we can make, are really game changers for us. I've noticed marketing today is hiring data scientists and people dedicated to analytics, and I think it's only a natural evolution that and employer or human resources will have a data science team that an really understand all the information about the company, about the brand, about the reputation, and can really provide the feedback loop going back to search engines. It can really change the company and understand what needs to be fixed. Yes, I'm a big fan of data science. I think we've just scratched the top of the surface. I think engineering and tech companies are leading the charge, marketing is closely after that, but I think human resources, like that's where the game changers are going to be because if you can convince the CEO and executives to change bit from data, then companies get better and there's a lot more great companies to go and work for.

Excellent Steve. I've been waiting on this one…Does Glassdoor use their own internal employee generated data to improve your company?

Yes. Absolutely. In fact we use it not only for employees, but people that interview at the company. We religiously practice what we preach. Any person that comes for an interview, we ask them to post feedback, and we do get feedback on where we have to make changes. It's not perfect, and we haven't cracked the code to be the ultimate perfect company for interviewing. There was recent feedback that was shared among the executives and as a result people were told, we need to change, and this is what needs to happen. We took it really like; we went like, "Really, this actually happened in an interview?" And yes, hiring managers respond to interview reviews and we take it seriously.

> *"The message was sent out clear, if you're hiring someone you dedicate your full time to them, you treat them special, they've made time for you."*
>
> —STEVE BURTON,
> GLASSDOOR

To give an example, this is being transparent, one person was interviewing for us and that person was on their mobile phone, not giving the candidate their full attention. That's totally unacceptable. The message was sent out clear, if you're hiring someone you dedicate your full time to him or her, you treat them special, they've made time for you. And that's what we learned from that interview feedback. Yes. We want to improve and wanted to hear what we need to fix. The faster you can make the action and you can correct, the better we're going to be at hiring talent.

That goes for me anyway, it goes from politicians to leaders, to people that seem kind of untouchable, that just makes them more human and it's like, "Okay, they do the same things that I do."

That to me, I think, organizationally is where companies can take away, when they get a chance to listen to it, because I know every single person will download this, and then take a listen at some point in time, and so, I love the fact that just course correcting and creating a culture of, "It's all right to make a mistake, but don't do it over and over again. Fix it. That's the biggest thing. If it's not acceptable to do, but mistakes happen, for whatever reason, as bad as they can be, and you just don't tend to do it, or you're going to put yourself and your career at risk because you're affecting the brand, and you're affecting people's lives, especially in the interview process.

Yes Bryan, absolutely. We want to grow the company and we can't grow without hiring people, and if people come in and they're not happy, that impacts their ability to grow the company.

Steve, what's the most critical point, if you can distill it down, that you see, just in your experience, and also within the data, and being in marketing, what's the most critical point in the interview process?

I think it's going into the interview and preparing, and really understanding who is the company, what do they do, what do employees currently think about working at the company, and where is my opportunity in that company. I think you could ask the tough questions in the interview, and normally if the employer interviewing the candidate, and going through the history, I think jobseekers today, when they've got this wealth of information and they see something that might be a red flag, they have every right to challenge the employer and ask them the tough questions so that they can feel confident in going to that job, that my expectations are aligned and I can be successful. I actually think preparing for the interview and doing your research and really understanding the employer, and its more the jobseeker interviewing the employer these days because the wealth of talent is so huge everyone's fighting for the right people. But yes, we've had employees tell us, people bring print ads to the Glassdoor reviews to the interview and will actually put their finger on the interview saying, can you explain why this happened in the company. Yes. It's power to the people. They're not afraid to say something [laughter].

Don MacPherson, Modern Survey
Wearable Technology Is Coming

Welcome our guest, Mr. Don MacPherson, President of Modern Survey.

Thanks, Bryan. Thanks for having me on today.

So, I want to kick it off, but I want to get it going with—you just took a very quick trip to Norway, and I want you to tell us, first of all, the single most interesting thing, anything that surprised you about Norway, and then we'll come back around to some of your travels because you have quite the dossier of traveling that I find fascinating, and I think it's very important relative to when you're looking at culture, and you're looking at data for a company, I think the well-roundedness adds another perspective. But anyway, the most interesting thing that you saw in Norway that maybe surprised you a little bit. Or intrigued you, either one.

Bryan, well Norway was country number 63 for me, and I had a Friday off and a Monday off, so I thought well, I'll fly out Thursday evening, get there Friday, spend all day Friday, Saturday, and Sunday there, and fly back on Monday, and so it was a whirlwind trip. I went alone. I had a couple nights hotel booked, and no other plans besides that, and so what I saw in Norway were a few things. Number one, Oslo was about as clean a city as you can imagine. Very safe, and one of the most interesting and compelling things was I saw a $100,000 Tesla taxi cab, and I thought well that's pretty interesting, you don't see that every day. And that's $100,00 US, so who knows how much it cost over in Norway, but that was one of the most interesting things. I also had an opportunity to see the Peace Museum, where they have a museum honoring the Nobel Peace Prize winners, which is handed out in Oslo every year in October, so those were a couple of the highlights.

Well, those are definitely two outstanding highlights I might add. I would definitely enjoy seeing both of those, multiple times, that's fantastic. 63 countries. That is one of the things that, I know we have known each other for several years, and one of the things that I never get tired of hearing about, quite frankly. Because that's one of those things to me that's just, I mean, that's one of your passions is traveling the globe. Will probably travel to space if you have the opportunity in you lifetime just to be able to experience it, so you are kind of a modern day explorer. Not too many of those around, so it's a privilege to hear the stories that come out of your travels.

Bryan well, thanks, and space has been on my mind. You know, Richard Branson has his company that is exploring bringing civilians up into space, and I've thought about it. It's a little pricey now, at $200,000, so I might save that for a few years, but it's crossed my mind once or twice.

Don, tell us a little bit about your company, and after that, kind of jump into why you think data is even relevant. We will start right at the top of the mountain with the questions.

Well, data is relevant because we are a data company. Modern Survey measures the employee life cycle. So, we measure how effectively people are on-boarded into their organization, how engaged they are, how they are performing, how effective their leaders are, and opinions of employees as they are leaving the organization. So, those are the five different metrics that we measure, and we've got a performance management solution, and engagement solution, onboarding effectiveness solution, all of these things are things that we measure. And based on the measurement, we are able to determine how the organization is going to perform, how individuals are going to be able to perform, and how teams are going to be able to perform. And we are able to integrate the data so the pool, the greater pool of data can be more meaningful. These datasets don't have to live in silos.

So, that's what we do every day. We help our clients determine the likelihood that people are going to stay with their organization, how they are going to perform, and then the last thing that we do is we have a business intelligence platform called Heat, so we are measuring the employee life cycle, but then Heat brings all of your key performance indicators together. Not only your employee data, but your customer data, your financial performance, those types of things, and even things that are pre-hire, like applicant tracking data and Heat brings it all together to help create not only predictive metrics, but also dashboards and business intelligence reporting.

Don, two parts to the question. Where do you see people starting to get the use of data right? Because it's still, you know, we're still in the infancy in terms of broader use, in my opinion. Please feel free to disagree and say I have a different take on it. I'm good with that. And the second part of the question is where do you see people not quite getting it right, or getting it wrong?

Bryan, well, the first part of your question is where are people getting it right? And the people who get it right, or the organizations who get it right start with a problem in mind. So, if you are working with data, you need to ask yourself, what is our problem. So, for example, you're a large organization, and you are losing 25% of your sales force annually. That's a problem. The industry average is 10%. We know we have a problem here. Now, why? Let's determine why this is. Why we are 15 percentage points above the average, and you can have all sorts of data to help you tell that story, but where people get it wrong—as you asked—is they just put together a bunch of information, a bunch of data. They know they have data about employees, about customers, they have financial data, they've got all sorts of data, and they just think they can put it into a pot, mix it together, and come up with some sort of conclusion about the organization. That's not the way big data works. That's not the way data scientists think about solving problems. You have to have that problem in mind, and a way to structure the data in order to solve that problem. So, that's where people get it right, and that's where people get it wrong.

So Don, relative to the employee life cycle, is there any area that if you were starting into becoming a data driven company and culture, that you would advise people to jump into first on the data collection?

Where we see a lot of organizations, Bryan, starting is by measuring employee engagement. We know that employee engagement is very predictive of employee performance; we know it is predictive of safety, quality, retention, all sorts of very positive things, customer satisfaction, and ultimately profitability and the ability to grow the organization. So, that's where a lot of organizations start, and employee engagement has become very affordable, and very actionable as well, as long as an organization is asking the right questions. So, most organizations, if they are over 100 employees, can do a very affordable, very valuable employee engagement survey. And where we are seeing organizations graduate to after they have done the employee engagement survey is start to measure things like onboarding effectiveness. So, when an organization is bringing in new people into the organization, they are measuring how well people are being welcomed into the organization, how effectively they are being trained, how they are being empowered to do their jobs. And we do it typically at 7, 30, and 90 days.

So, when a new employee starts, at 7 days we do their first survey, at 30 days, and then at 90 days. And then we integrate that data with the engagement data, so if somebody has broadened the organizations effectively, what is the likelihood they are going to be fully engaged. Well, the likelihood is going to be very high, according to our research, but what if someone is not on-boarded effectively? Well, we've identified one question that is highly predictive of somebody leaving the organization, and that is when the job is not as expected. If you responded on the onboarding survey, my job is not as expected, you are almost three times more likely to leave the organization in the first year than somebody who was sold the appropriate job, or the job that was as expected, and so that's where a lot of organizations take it after engagement. They start doing onboarding surveys, and then the last thing that they take on, or the third thing—so, engagement, and then onboarding—is exit. Tying the onboarding data and engagement data with retention data. And those three things, most organizations are able to number one, understand act on, understand, and afford. And those are the things that kind of start down this big data path.

Don, has Modern Survey reviewed at how consumer data is looked at? Then tried to use some of the best practices or methodology around buying patterns, why people buy this, and then buy that, or take something back?

Well, in terms of patterning, the way we look at data, not necessarily, but in terms of integrating the employee data with customer data, absolutely. That's a big part of what we look at, and there are some industries that lend themselves toward doing this very effectively. So, for example in a retail environment, let's say you've got a retail company with 1,000 stores, and we have employee data about those stores, we've got customer data about those stores, and we've got financial data about those stores. That is a very rich environment for being able to tie and make the business case for effective management of employees, effective engagement of employees, because we know, and it makes perfect sense, that the more engaged people are, the better they are going to perform, the better service they are going to provide customers or clients, depending on what your terminology is, and when those customers or clients are appropriately served, getting quality goods, getting quality services, they are going to spend more and that store is going to grow.

So, we are very interested in looking at how those three different data pools work together—the employee data pool, the customer data pool, and then finally the financial data pool. And retail really lends itself to that, the same with retail banking or large scale banking where you've got many self-contained stores or locations.

Don, where are we at 10 years from now relative to this big data conversation? What are we going to be talking about that you feel is different?

Ten years from now Bryan, I have no idea, to be honest with you. I can give you a very good idea of what it looks like 2 or 3 years from now, or at least where we think things are going to go. Not surprisingly, we see social as very important to the big data conversation, so one of the things that our research has found is that only 34% of the US workforce follows their company on social media, and that's going to change. That's going to change dramatically. Social is going to be the way that CEOs and executives communicate with their employees about the future of the organization, about initiatives, about product development, about all sorts of things like that. And it doesn't have to be Facebook or LinkedIn or Twitter, or things that are very transparent to the outside, but it can be internal social platforms as well.

So, we know that's going to be very important, and just to give you some context, it's only 34% of the US workforce following their companies. With Millennial population, it's 45%, boomers it's only 25%. And so as more Millenials come into the workplace, social is going to become more and more important. They are going to be following their organizations, and as more CEOs start to communicate that way, it will become a very important way of reaching employees. If you have a job, you have a phone. If you have a phone, you have access to these different social platforms. Now, that's just communication, but imagine being able to understand employees' sentiment, and being able to take that data and understand how employees feel about the company, and how that relates to their ability to be retained as an employee. We see social as being very important to the future of big data on the employee side of things. The other side of things is wearables, and I'll touch on that in a moment, but social we see as very, very critical for understanding employee behavior and understanding employee retention.

Don I've been waiting and love the conversation about wearables. I'm literally right down the street from Garmin, here in Kansas City.

You want to jump into wearables Bryan?

Oh yeah lets do it Don!

Bryan, that's always an interesting one, and it's where we are putting a lot of attention moving forward. We think that the social piece will be something that is widely adopted in the next couple of years. In fact, in 2014, we spent a lot of research and development, and we released something called Heat Social, so we've got this business intelligence platform called Heat, and 2014 we released Heat Social, and it's where we absorb information from social media platforms, like Glassdoor, Facebook, LinkedIn, Twitter, etc. This year we are focusing on absorbing data from wearable technologies for health and wellness wearables. You know, FitBit, Jawbone Up, these different wearables that people are wearing for personal use, we see a very important application to business use as well. And so we are focused on the health and wellness for now, but going forward, it's going to work itself into safety, it's going to work itself into a number of way that we can evaluate performance, and right now, from a health and wellness perspective, we are trying to understand how active people are, how that influences their level of engagement, how that influences their happiness, how that influences how they feel about the organization, and also how important a health and wellness program is to an organization.

So, being able to understand how active people are, and how they are adopting their health and wellness plan will become more and more important, particularly as healthcare costs go up. And then in terms of just evaluating performance—this is something that I learned not too long ago that blew me away. So, I'm a big basketball fan, I love the NBA, I love college basketball, and I found out that there are uniforms that have embedded wearable technologies in them, and it tracks body movements of, say, basketball players. So, you know, if one basketball player is going to his left and shooting a shot, maybe his is 40% effective, he hits 40% of those shots going to his left, but when he goes to his right, he is 60% effective, he hits 60% of his shots.

This is data that these wearable technologies are able to capture and report back on performance. Now, that is remarkable to me that these uniforms are able to track that information and relate it directly to an individual's performance. That is going to be pervasive in the work-place of the future. So, imagine 2 or 3 years from now—in fact, there is a company based out of Boston called SocioMetrics, and they have this badge. This badge captures data about interactions that we have with other employees. So, it can determine based on our voice inflections, based on our tone, based on the other individuals' voice feedback, if we are friendly with one another, if we are adversarial, how we are perform-ing in our jobs, it's capturing all sorts of data like that, and this is just the very beginning stages of the workplace of the future, but these sorts of wearable technologies will determine how effectively we perform, and that may sound very Big Brother-like, but it's coming, and it's probably coming sooner than you think. Probably not 10 years, probably more like 2 to 3 years from now.

Don, our buddy Tiger Woods probably needs to embed some things in his uniform to figure out what's going on when it feels right and when it doesn't because that's so movement driven on a regular basis. Everything is off at the moment, and so anyway, not to digress too far on that. By the way, to everybody listening, Don not only loves basketball, but he shot some mean hoops in his day, now that we have to put you out to pasture, but you played pro in Europe, is that correct?

Wow, it's been 20 years ago Bryan, believe it or not, this year, I returned from Germany. So, it's been 20 long years and I haven't played in about 4 or 5 years, so it is back in the day, certainly.

Don it's a great, you've got a great perspective on it. A lot of years of training went into that and studying the craft. I'm a huge fan. I think that's one of the next frontiers relative to that live data. There is so much that can be gleaned from that related to happiness, like satisfaction, happiness, fulfillment, I think there's a lot to do with that. Health and wellness, I mean I can see—I've never really thought about that, but I could see that there is an amazing amount of information that can be tied all the way down to your key performance indicators that you potentially could figure out. Like, there are some things that you need a group that is just more active than others. Maybe others, there is no relevance to it. You can't draw any correlations that are positive relative to performance, but there might be some groups where you're like wow, this is really a driver of this silo, or this subset within a company, right?

Because there is not one culture, I don't know this is a question I guess. Do you see there is one company culture that really drives everything, or is there just a bunch of these little culture pods that eventually bubble up and cumulatively create the culture? Which way do you see it, or how do you see it?

Bryan, I often see it as very leadership-centric, so leadership creating the culture and the culture becoming pervasive throughout the organization. On occasion, when it's a very geographically disperse organization, you will have different bubbles of culture popping up, but that's not necessarily the healthiest unless the culture at the top is diseased, broken, then having some separate cultures bubbling up that are healthier can be worthwhile. I wanted to comment, just on the wearables for a moment because one of the things that you were mentioning is very important. We are going to be able to draw all sorts of conclusions and be able to use wearables to predict behavior and performance in the future, but

I will say, after using a wearable technology to measure heart rate, to measure my performance in the gym. The most important aspect of that technology was awareness, and when people are using these wearable technologies, they will get a greater sense of self-awareness, which will lead to introspection, and eventually, improved performance. That can't be understated. It may sound very, very simple, but there is great power in having employees throughout an organization being far more aware of themselves, aware of their behavior, aware of their actions, and wearables will help provide us that in the workplace of the future.

Don, this is something I think and have published a book on so I'm a huge fan of that awareness-life cycle, you know, in life in general, and I completely agree with that. I have literally seen that happen, I have experienced it, just by introducing the ingredient of measuring something, you know, where you're tracking it and something is helping you be more aware, it definitely does heighten the fact like. It's simple, but it's powerful. And no everybody is ready to be self-aware, but I would say about 80% of us are. About 20% of us are going to be hesitant, I don't know, I don't want to know that. But about 80% of us do want to know how we are behaving, how that is going to affect our performance, and be held accountable, and hold ourselves accountable for that.

Brent Bannon, formerly Facebook

So Many Places You Could Go Wrong

Today we've got a fantastic guest, Brent Bannon, Dr. Brent Bannon—has degrees from two of my favorite schools on the planet and I'm only a little envious of that, but I've gotten past it. He's the founder of Learn Rig based out of Charleston, South Carolina, and former Research Manager of the growth team for our friends over at Facebook. He's worked with Growth Engagement in the mobile team at Facebook. He did a lot of things at Facebook, monetization, just general market research, and again, literally went to two of my favorite schools on the planet, Stanford, in lovely Palo Alto, and the London School of Economics in Political Science.

Bryan, I guess I started back understanding the data process probably while I was in Stanford in grad school doing political communication. I went there thinking I was going to be Josh Lyman from the West Wing. I ended up getting into some heavy kind of statistical stuff while I was there. I had a few different roles between then and now, but about five years ago I wound up at Facebook in the market research team looking at users, developers, advertisers, you name it, and I'd like to mention this, I'm going to take the time there as one of the monetization analytics team working a lot on actually small businesses on Facebook, to try to understand how the platform works.

The last couple years on the growth team doing a bunch of stuff, whether some kind of data plan the staff would put together from some survey programs that were really useful for understanding why people do things beyond just what they're doing. I was lucky enough to get involved with FacebookImplement.org, an initiative toward the end there so were trying to understand what are the barriers to increment adoption in the developing world, people who've never really had access to the internet, how can we pave the way to get those guys online, and how can we use research to support that. It was a pretty interesting journey. And then about a year ago I moved back to Charleston. I'm here in sunny Charleston this morning. Then the company that I founded for the most part just been doing consulting work around growth and data, but I'm kind of at the start of my own startup venture now, continuing in that area of opening up connectivity and trying understand how I can use data to empower people and encourage people to get online and seek out the opportunities that they might not otherwise have had.

Brent, that is a fascinating career. You've been at the one of the highest, obviously one of the most noted and data heavy organizations on the planet that's ever existed. Just an incredible time to do what you're doing, and so totally excited about that. I love that you've worked for other places, but I'm pretty sure that people are going to listen to the show because of your Face-book experience. So, we're going to concentrate a little on that. We're going to deal in reality this morning. And I also pegged you as Josh first time I met you by the way, so I think you got there, you maybe didn't realize it on the political communications front.

What was the thing that surprised you the most about data at our friends at Facebook Brent?

Yes. I think one of the things that, and I've interviewed a lot of people for positions there as well, there's a lot of excitement about this huge data set that they have there. I think one of the things for me was the fact, at the time I joined they were probably somewhere around the fourth or five hundred million user mark, and that's a lot of data coming in on an ongoing basis and people are always kind of impressed at the scale. I talk to a lot of people who are salivating at the prospect of what you can do with this data. I think one of the things that surprised me was even at that scale there's a lot of sparseness in the data. There are a lot of actions that aren't taken universally even among that many people there are only a few people doing certain actions. An example of that would be thinking about social context, so at the time that I was there the ad leads were pre-mobile ads, or the ads were like the little white hand sign ads. They were doing a lot of experimenting with the social context there. Like if you have a friend who likes this page when they run the ad, then you've shown this person likes this page.

There was a lot of opportunity there. You think about if I'm learning an ad for music verses something to do with cars, there are different frames of mind that would have more or less influence in the way I think about those areas. I remember thinking about this, like if we could just figure out who are the people who are the people most likely to influence you about these things we can probably make these ads more effective by showing different specific people there. Well, it turns out at the time liking a page wasn't a very common activity. And a lot of people liked one or two pages, but not much beyond that. You didn't have tons of people liking all kinds of pages kind of showing all the stuff that they liked. So, it turns out for any given ad that we showed somebody we might only have one or two people that we know who like that page. You're not using data to do an optimization to understand who is the most influential person, or any of that kind of thing. You're basically just showing the person that's there. I ran into instances where the opposite was true as well.

I remember looking at, I think it was Coca Cola, had one of the biggest pages at the time in terms of the number of people who liked the page. I wanted to get a feel for how likely you were to like the Coca Cola page dependent on whether anybody else you knew liked them. It turned out it was really hard to find any people in America who didn't have at least one friend who liked that page. So we [laughter] ended with some pretty sophisticated—we used propensity score matching to create a model that would basically make a pseudo control group that we could compare to people who did have, who were connected to people who liked the Coca Cola page, which is kind of a nice little statistical trick after the fact to look at it. It comes to not how you want to go about answering that question in the first place, but it was just one of those things where you realized that there are some things that are going on huge scale, to find the people who aren't doing that is actually quite hard.

Then there are other cases where just trying to find people who are doing something that you care about is actually pretty hard as well. Even at a billion users you have, there are definitely things that I was interested in that when I would go to look at it it was pretty hard to find enough volume of people doing it to really dig into that stuff.

Yes, that kind of blows your mind when you have that much data and you still have a degree of specificity that challenges how you're looking at the data. I think that's amazing when you start talking about that much data and then when you trickle it down to much smaller data sets in comparison, how much more difficult that's going to get.

Brent, would you approach that differently, two parts to the question, would you approach the data a little differently if, for example, today it seems like a lot of people now like a lot more pages. From what you're saying, back when you started a few years ago people liked a handful of pages. Now people like tons and tons, and tons of pages, from just anecdotally it looks that way. The two parts of the question is, 1. How would you approach it now that everybody likes so many more pages? And 2. What do you think has changed in people's behaviors?

Yes Bryan. That's an interesting question. Just for full disclosure I haven't looked at liking activity in a good couple of years so I'm not really sure what the situation is, but it's –

Hypothetical. We'll go with hypothetical.

Yes. It's kind of an interesting problem Bryan. I think the first thing is just by having it, if you take the contention that people just like more pages, then I think any kind of analysis you want to do with that existing data becomes so much easier just because you've kind of got over the threshold where you're already working with a mass of data where you can find significant differences between groups that do like the pages and don't like the page, or other activities that might be correlated with that, which is just really hard to do when you're essentially talking about a rare event.

> *"First of all there's a ton of places you could go wrong, anywhere from selecting the wrong significant models to just violating some assumptions and all this kind of stuff."*
> —DR. BRENT BANNON, FORMERLY OF FACEBOOK

The interesting thing that kind of lines up with this in that context is that liking a page is like the technical intellect that actually represents some underlying preference. You're actually using this as a proxy in some ways from what people actually like in the real world. It depends on what kind of question you're interested in. If you're interested in something around people's preferences then you now have a much stronger signal. I actually think it gets a lot easier and gives you some much more straight-forward statistical techniques if you're looking at that kind of stuff. Look back on the question. But if you're actually thinking about how those interactions are related to other things that happen on the site which might be something that you'd be interested in as a researcher at Facebook. Then there's not a whole lot of difference, but the fastness of the kind of action in the past was basically part of the system you had to work within because if you're wondering around about what happens when you show somebody as social context because they've taken this action then you can only work with people who have taken that action.

Again it becomes a little easy when it's more common just because it's easier to get some significance around it to make comparisons between groups. But I think a lot of it is thinking about exactly what they're trying to learn from the data and being clear about the limitations are.

Where do you think people struggle when it comes to data Brent?

Bryan, this is kind of an interesting one. First of all there's a ton of places you could go wrong, anywhere from selecting the wrong significant models to just violating some assumptions and all this kind of stuff. But I think it kind of varies with the kind of skill set you're working on and the questions that you're looking at, but the thing that I run into a lot that I think is pretty common is struggling with sampling or representativeness, which is to say—an example of this would be, a lot of people talk about big data and they kind of assume that if they have this huge data set they can do whatever they want with it and it's going to be representative of whatever they care about just because they've got so much data. If you have a million data point's people are very confident in making generalizations from that to the world.

I think the problem is you can have this big data but it's not necessarily representative, but whoever it is you're trying to draw conclusions about—an example I've used from back in the day, when I was working at Facebook I used to see this quite a lot, external companies analyzing data from the public API and they would do this analysis, and they'd have millions and millions of loads of data and be very comfortable making generalizations about, this is what Facebook users are like. The problem with that was that the only data that came into the public API is stuff that people have posted and content people have produced that they were sharing publicly. So, it didn't include anything that was shared only among friends. And there are big differences between the kinds of people who are willing to share things with the public verses with their friends to friends to friends.

So, even though you have millions of loads of data, you've got like a sample of people who are using the site that are kind of different from the people that are missing in a way that skews your vote to make any kind of conclusions there. And I think this is pretty common even when people set out to do a primary research study at companies, I've seen people go out and, you know, whether it's convenient sampling or whether it's non-response rates that are just bias in the data, or whether you just took a big chunk, like it's pretty common for engineers working with the data to take a 1% sample to try to understand what's going on from the general point of view, but it's not always a really a true random sample, and there's artifacts in the data production process that means that the 1% sample you're looking at is not necessarily a true representation of the world, which often doesn't matter for the things that they first set out to look at, whether they're looking at technical metrics, or whether it's speed and reliability, but as you start trying to draw from the data sets there to make these better kind of inferences, I just think that gets really hard.

I mean we this case, we went out to the Philippines when I was working with the Internet.org guys trying to understand whether people could receive the marketing messages that they could places for free in this particular area and we were going after rural areas that there is no research position there outside of the sense of saving the environment, but the people we cared about were people out in the rural environments who weren't typically deemed heavy users of media or users of the internet at all, and understanding how you can sample those people, of course face to face, which is very different from the kind of big data, how do you mine this data you already have, but some of those questions about, how do you insure that the sample that you have is representative of the people that you're trying to draw conclusions about. I think those are just kind of common universal things that people struggle with and different researchers have different tolerances for how much they're willing to just take speed over ethics. I think that's just the challenge that everybody kind of deals with on an ongoing basis.

Definitely based on what you just shared, Brent, how do we position ourselves to get more informative results, which that to me is a very important question?

Yes, and I think one of the points here actually relates directly to the sampling and representative issue. I think you have to take the time and the effort upfront to actually articulate, who do you want to say something about? Who exactly do you want to learn something about? And then work backwards from there. You might want to know something only about people who use your product. You may actually only care about people who don't use your product yet. You may have some idea about some small faction of your user base that you actually want to grow. Those are the people in the sweet spot and you want to understand how do you people that. People that you have to come into find the people that you care about before you actually go down the path of being a researcher, and make sure that you are drawing your conclusions from an appropriate group that you can expand to people that you want to make generalizations about.

But actually I think even more fundamentally than that is kind of the defining the outcomes that you care about in order to make sure you're asking—let's forget the research question. Forget how you frame the research question, but what is the actual business question that you want to answer? Are you trying to understand how you can increase engagement, for example, and if you do want to increase engagement, how do you define that, what do you mean by engagement and increasing engagement. Do you mean you want more people to touch your product in a given month? Or do you mean you want to take people who are already using your product and you want them to touch the product every day? Or are you trying to change them and do you have some specific behavior in mind? If you start with that premise and then kind of try to build your research questions around, what are the proxies for the thing that I actually care about, I think you'll have a much better chance of success.

And what it also helps you do is get everybody on the same page upfront about how you're making definitions because it's pretty common for a researcher to make and say, "Hey, I found that people aren't dealing with things we care about." and a bunch of product managers kind of wave the hand and say, "Well, actually that's not a really good proxy for the things that we actually care about. We actually care about X and you're measuring Y." So, if you can get everybody on the same page before you travel down that path then have some kind of consensus on whatever it is you're trying to answer, then I think that [click] nine times out of ten that'll just pull you in a much better position from the start.

Brent, I know you played in the B2C world, then the B2B world and I think there's—because B2C is so much more established as far as understanding transactions and buying habits, and buying preferences, that's been looked at a lot longer. What's some of the stark contrasts or differences in similarities, I guess, but mainly key differences between working in B to C verses B to B data.

Yes. I think as a sweeping generalization and I'm going to kind of apply this to the tech world because when I worked in financial centers and some other industries that didn't necessarily hold that strongly, but in general the scale of data you can get in the B2C world is going to be larger if you have a product that is used by a lot of end consumers. So, there's some kind of—there's a point where it's a little easier to analyze that data because you've got so much in that data and you don't have to use as many kind of tricks to, I don't want to say tricks, but you'll have to take such a sophisticated methodology to actually get some useful insights pretty quickly in the B2C world, you're often dealing with more con—it depends on what you're talking about.

The transaction data that you're talking about for example, you can have huge data sets there and you're also dealing with companies that have a much higher content level for fairly sophisticated ways of looking at that data. But if you then run in, let's say small businesses you can kind of blow that out and have fairly large data sets, but there's a potential difference in the ordinance for the data, and their level of sophistication. When I worked with small businesses one of the things we were trying to do was prove out the case, how do we prove out ad effectiveness for small businesses? If you think about big businesses, you know, consumer package goods, financial services, these guys who are used to this and they have teams to do this kind of research, you can go to write a white paper, like its own technical report that uses regression model and a bunch of other stuff to explain the value of ads. And those guys are comfortable talking about it in those terms, but if you go to the mom and pop bakery or something like that, these guys don't have the time to digest a 30 page technical paper, they don't necessarily see themselves as being similar enough to those businesses that they can actually buy into the method you're using, so you might have more data, but you're constrained to putting together an analysis that is, that if you had communicated this communication constraint where the bigger issue is not necessarily the data and what you could theoretically do with the data. It's what you can do in a way that you can talk about it that kind of resonates with the audience there. I think, actually, the other challenge in a lot of cases in the B2C world is that you're taking data that represents, whether its actions, behaviors, or opinions of individuals and you're kind of extrapolating to the motivation of the organization.

I worked at a financial services firm where we surveyed a bunch of our customers, could be anybody from McNamara to a small credit union, and you might have 15 people touching the product from a large national bank, you might have only one person touching a personal credit union, and you're trying to extrapolate from those different kinds of data to say something about what motivates the company that is buying the product, and you kind of have this data that somewhat incomplete because the person who's touching the product might not actually be the person who is deciding to buy the product or kind of driving the strategy around the product as well. So, there's a bunch of stuff where, in the

B2B world, you're not necessarily dealing directly with a similar kind of contact that represents them.

The next question Brent is one that will get a lot of people's attention and probably some release of tension possibly. How do we relate data to growth?

Yes, this is obviously close to my interest kind of being the research guy who's in a global team. It's interesting because I think people talk about growth in a lot of different ways, they really can use a bunch of different stuff, in some cases they might learn a specific approach doing AB tests, or like SEO and SEM, and search engine optimization, and email, and all these other tools. But I think it really boils down—for me it boils down to a couple of things. It's user acquisition, or customer acquisition, and retentions. One is how do you get people to use the things you're making? And the other is, once you've got them to try the product, how do you keep them engaged to keep them around?

I think the interesting thing is that, to me, growth is kind of a methodology almost in itself, and it could be anything from you running an AB test, to optimizing the number of people who convert through a new user experience flow, or how many people actually are willing to try—the contacting portal would be something at Facebook that we can do testing around. But it might be a couple of surveys as well. You want to go that step further, you want to try to understand why people are doing the things that they're doing, not just why they're doing them. You can be using customer surveys, you might even be bringing people into a lab and having them play with new versions of the product to try to understand what works and what doesn't work. But again I think the interesting things are around knowing what the outcome is that you're optimizing for and how can you find that kind of the best and again, in the tech world the test doesn't matter as well as the optimizer. And it can be really small operations, if you think about signing new people up for some kind of internet service, if you have hundreds of thousands of people coming and hitting new user experience flow, as potential signers, if you can make a tenth of the percent or two tenths of a percent difference on how many people actually make it through to the end and actually sign up for an account, over time that's actually pretty huge.

And so, a lot of it is chipping away these little things and making places easier for people to go through and to get to, and who's using friction. And using data to understand there's a lot of data inherent in all of this, whether it's looking at the percentage of people who convey it through some flow, or whether it's after the fact understanding of what people are doing with the site, or the product, or whatever you're working on, and just having a healthy understanding of what is the end goal you're trying to optimize for, and in this case it's normally acquisition of retention, and how do you use data to shed light on which things are working and pushing you towards that goal. So, to me growth is pretty much all about data.

Right. Brent is it possible to be too focused on data?

Yes, I actually believe this point and I talk to a lot of researchers who are pretty interested in any kind of question that comes our way that's interesting and they want to come and examine it. I've said no a lot in my professional life to taking on projects. I think it depends on what your objectives are. I think if you're trying to create a beautiful design oriented experience that's different than if your goal is to get a million people to do—if your core culture of your company and the things that you're trying to do are about putting something new out into the world, then I don't necessarily think you want to be completely led by data. And it's also a question of resources because usually there is some data, if you're going to spend time researching one thing you're not spending that time doing something else. To my way of thinking if something is relatively small on the grand scheme of your product and you have an experienced product manager there I'd say, let them use their instincts and their intuition. They'll have a good idea about what's going to work. And true, you should measure it so you understand if it's going to work, but for a lot of the time I would say, that's why you hire people like that, to drive that stuff, and there are a lot of places where this should just be using more intuition.

I mean you also have to have a culture that doesn't punish mistakes. You learn about the mistake and you recover from it and move on. But I think it is possible to get too trapped into this analysis paralysis process where you're obsessing about every decision, who needs this data and a lot of times that can slow you down and you won't—the best thing might be to take the acquisitions you think you can take and, you can roll it back later, you can always adjust course if you need to, but it's not always the best thing to wait, the length of time you need to wait for that data to shed light on everything. So, I definitely think it's possible to be too focused on the data.

Brent, what's a book you've read lately you want to tell us about, one, and two, who's your football allegiance? You can pick the order.

I'll start with the book then. I just finished reading The Book Thief. They also made a movie out of it, if you want to check the movie option you can take that. I've actually seen the movie now as well and it's actually a good adaptation. It's about a young girl in Nazi Germany and she's kind of in an adopted family and they take in a Jewish guy and they simply hide him. Everything revolves around this set up and it's just a really good book. It's actually, I think technically a kids book, but I got a lot out of it, especially I have a young daughter, so there was a lot in this book that resonated, and it was really good. I'd highly recommend it, like I said, but the movie is a good adaptation, so, do check that out if you don't have time to read the book.

On the football front I'm a Geordie, born and raised in New Castle so my team is New Castle United. It's not necessarily something I'm proud of right now [laughter], but they're having a pretty disastrous run. They've got all kinds of problems off the pitch as well. I think we're going to finish middle of the table at the end. There's just a lack of ambition there right now. But yes, it's been a painful few years in football life.

Naomi Bloom

The History of Big Data

I want to welcome Naomi Bloom. Welcome to Thug Metrics Naomi.

Bryan, thank you so much for having me.

Well and I typically do a little bit of an intro but you've been around too long and you've done too many things for me to try and do an introduction. So if you would be so kind to introduce yourself and what's important to you and then we'll jump in with maybe a little history of big data from your perspective. I think that's a great place to start.

Great Bryan. Well when you've had a very long career it's hard to summarize it in thirty words or less but I guess I've evolved from an early, my early career was as a software programmer when we were first starting to automate HR and what was then called personnel administration and payroll. I did that for about 10 years, programmer, analyst, project manager, head of computer operations at a number of different places both scientific and business computing. I spent nine years as a partner with a major consultancy, American Management Systems, back in the day. We built custom software and implemented packaged software. I started and ran consulting practices but from 1987 forward I've been solo and worked with lots and lots of global fortune 500 companies on their HR strategy and by extension their HR technology strategy and then spent probably the last 10 years working predominately with the vendor community because it's all well and good to want to do something as an end user but if the technology's not there to do it, very few corporations have the wherewithal to go it alone.

Some of your listeners may know that as of the end of last year I put aside my direct client consulting work. I moved from consultant to what I like to think of as kibitzer so I'm still out there trying to keep it honest, writing and speaking but I'm not doing any more direct client consulting work.

Well I'm glad you didn't retire and hang it up for good. You're a great voice and I've just always enjoyed your perspective as well as thousands and thousands of other people so. Let's jump right into it. So if you could, give us a little bit of background from your perspective on kind of the term big data. So maybe start with a definition. Let's get some definitions from you of what big data really is and then maybe a little history.

Bryan, I think in order to talk about data we have to back up just a little bit and talk about why we should even care about it whether it's big, small or otherwise. What is it that matters because then when we talk about big data we're really ratcheting up for what is that matters. We never cared about data per say except obviously for compliances and things you have to do but it was never about data per say but what we could do with it and the thing we've always been trying to do with it even if we didn't describe it this way was to drive and improve business outcomes. In order to do that we had to somehow get decision makers to make better decisions because whether those decisions are made at a completely automated fashion as they increasingly are or they're made by actually human beings to inform that decision making so that the decisions are better. Inform it with data; inform it with better computational algorithms.

The whole point is better decisions driving better outcomes and it's not just that you need the data. You need to know what to do with it. So from the beginning, from the earliest, earliest uses of the abacus, you know from caveman counting how many animals they killed that day, from the very beginning of data it's always been trying to improve the outcomes. Well the term big data probably started in the early nineties. It was coincident with some activity in the commercial sphere where companies like Amazon which was founded in the 1994; Netflix came along in '97, Google in '98, Salesforce.com in '99. As these firms began to build architectures for dealing with the amount of data that was just a byproduct of their normal business they realized that they could not use classic relational database management systems, classic analytical tools that was just too much data and so one important aspect of the term big data when it's used properly is that it does not lend itself to data management with traditional technologies.

So I can tell all of your listeners, if they are applying the term big data or a vendor is applying the term big data, to data on their company managed in a traditional relational database management system it by definition is not big data. It may be more data than they ever managed before but it doesn't make it big, capital B. There are some good definitions of big data running around out there. One that I particularly like is one that defines it in terms of a set of characteristics. Those characteristics are the volume, the variety, the velocity, that's how fast it's being generated and moved around, how fast it's being changed, the variability.

When we deal with structured data as we do in traditional human resource management systems we know that if the field is gender and we have allowed for, I'm going to say six or eight different, different values because we're long past the point where we're dealing with traditional male and female. Nonetheless that there is a finite set of values, of valid values but when I have Twitter data, if I'm looking and trying to extract meaning from the flow of date from the Twitter-verse, we know that the terminology that's being used is completely unstructured and you and I might use very different terms to mean exactly the same thing and that variety brings its own set of challenges. Complexity is another dimension. When you take all of this together, there's almost no way that a single company, you know company X, is going to deal with big data in the human resource management space as regards to their own data. So I don't care if you're Wal-Mart and you have, I don't know how many employees they have let's say it's a million, if I have a million employee records and I'm paying people every two weeks and I'm having a certain amount of transaction volume with address changes and benefit enrollments and so on, that is not big data.

A good exception to that would be a company like ADP which is managing data on behalf of hundreds of thousands of companies and as you all know when they publish their analysis of new jobs added in the industry and in the U.S., when they publish their jobs data what they're doing is aggregating data across all of those companies and they're not just doing it with a traditional relational database system. They are getting into big data because of that aggregation across lots and lots of companies but where an individual company begins to get into big data is if in addition to traditional human management, talent management, payroll, benefits, etc., data, let's say they start studying the social exhaust for their own employees using an in-house social network of some flavor. That begins to get there because you're starting to have a little bit more unstructured data.

If it's widely used it's starting to generate information more quickly. If they start using technologies that can extract meaning from the flow of all the emails in the company again we're getting a different type of data, more unstructured, the velocity is greater because there's a constant flow of it. Starting to get towards big data have to have some new ways of managing it but if you now start tracking the social exhaust of your employees across all those external social networks, what they're doing on Twitter, when did they last update on LinkedIn, what are they having to say about your company in various online forums, now we're getting into big data.

So all the major commercial social websites that' we all use, Facebook and Twitter and so on, all of them are applying big data technology analytical techniques to our collective social exhaust and there's a really big important point here. When the term SaaS was first coined it meant something very specific and Bryan if your readers read my blogs at all they'll know that I stick to a very precise definition of SaaS but in today's world in HRM space every vendor is calling whatever the hell they've got, cloud or SaaS, they're using those terms almost interchangeably and half the time they're just hosting old stuff. The same thing has happened with the big data. It used to mean something very specific, very precise, and very rigorous. Increasingly everybody and their mother-in-law are describing whatever they're doing in analytics as big data.

Great Naomi. So, based on what you just shared what comes to mind to me is now we're in this tidal wave of kind of people understanding and wading into kind of data analytics, data intelligence even trying to understand what their data looks like, even what questions to ask which is the most important usually. So how does somebody marry up kind of a strategic intuition like where you want to go, what you want your products to do, with kind of your data intelligence because you have kind of subjective, kind of the art with the skill. How do you start to marry that question up, if you're an executive with you know with an organization?

Well let's start with a very simple example Bryan, and then sort of expand upon it. One of the first things that lots of companies do when they start thinking about analytics is and I'm talking here not about the kind of reports that told us you know our head count report or our you know our report on upcoming performance reviews that might be due or might be behind schedule. Not talking about that. I'm talking about the kinds of information that we want to use that drive decision making and one of the sort of first, let's call it more sophisticated things that companies try to do is really understand across their workforce both who is important to the firm and of the people who are important, what is their flight risk and by important I mean either that they're filling a role which is critical that is a role which directly drives business outcomes, could be a sales role but not necessarily or they're important because of their potential.

They are a name successor and even though today they may be running our Latin American sales support operation or customer support operation, they're really being groomed for a much longer-term role; we've invested a lot in them. So a person can be important either because of their role they fill today and the importance of that role or, and or I should say, because they have the kind of potential that we are grooming for bigger things along the progression of the firm. When we look at those kinds of individuals and those kinds of positions which we know how to identify when we ask ourselves the question about flight risk, what we're really saying is, is there something going on here which raises the possibility that this individual is going to leave us and leave us voluntarily and fairly soon.

If we're only looking at our own data that is the HRMS data that we have in a typical structured database we would look data, how is this person compensated compared to others doing similar work, have they had frequent increases, is there something about the nature that they're doing today that puts pressure on families or a lot of heavy travel involved. Is this an individual who has had not enough promotions or too many reassignments or a bunch of other things that we could intelligently ask? Assuming we could formulate an algorithm which taking that information into consideration could give us some prediction and that's not a foolish thing to do but it's nothing to do with big data.

If we want to really look at that same question, flight risk from more of a big data perspective not we have to look at other kinds of information. Everybody teases about the fact that the first thing someone does when they're looking for new opportunity is they update their LinkedIn profile and that is perhaps true of lower to mid-level workers but it's not true of executives. That is not what they do. The first thing they do is spend more time networking with colleagues and the only way you'd know that is by looking at their calendar which might be in outlook and therefore could be pulled in as information. Looking at their calendar to see how many lunch appointments are they doing. If they've been doing an average of three external lunch appointments a month and it suddenly jumps to 10, something's cooking.

Another thing we might look at is in that particular role; let's say the role is CIO, what's the average turnover period, the elapsed time in that role across the industry that we're in or across the geography that we're in or across the other characteristics of our situation. Now we're looking at external data and we're bringing it into and marrying it with internal data. What about this person's social exhaust, have they gone from being fairly inactive on Twitter to getting very active, have they suddenly started a blog or have they always had a blog in which they wrote about things that were relevant to our industry and now they're really writing about big ideas in IT, big ideas in digital transformation. Who are they hanging out with, you know, have they suddenly added a bunch of connections to people who are maybe in the analyst community, maybe in the venture community? So it doesn't get to big data just because we're calculating by an algorithm flight risk. It gets to big data because we're using not just internal available data and structured data but we're really casting a much wider net and once we do that we have to have some way of managing that data and we're not going to bring it in to some silly relational database. That just won't do the trick.

I could take that thought process with a number of other critical analytics. We're trying to answer questions like, which should we hire and that question is really part of the bigger question of who should we hire to get the best possible business results. If I'm looking at 20 candidates for a given role, again perhaps that same CIO role, how do I know a priori which of those candidates is the most likely to really help improve the business outcomes of the company? I can do that from an internal focus. I can do that with a broad, cast the big net, big data perspective and increasingly we're taking that second perspective and we should be.

Naomi, from an algorithm building perspective and thinking about it a different way because like you, to your point an executive is different than middle management is different than hourly relative to where you're starting to lose people and trying to be a little more predictive of that so great, great practical thought process around that, that I'm sure a lot of people hadn't really tended to think through.

Bryan, you know there's another angle on this, which I think is important to your readers, to your listeners, excuse me. If I am purveyor, if I'm a vendor of HR technology and that might be talent management, that might be something in sourcing, it might be co-HRMS, if I'm a vendor and I have real SaaS, blooming SaaS as I like to think of it as I build up an install base as I have more and more customers which of course is what I'm trying to do I begin to have tremendous power in the aggregated data of two different kinds. In the first instance I have the aggregated data on how that software's being used, every click, swipe, poke your nose at the screen, I've got them all and as a vendor I can draw tremendous insight from that, that helps me build better software, correct user experience challenges, build out functionality in areas where there's a lot of configuration activity and I could make it easier, I could deliver more in that particular area to look at features that really aren't being used and perhaps put less emphasis on building those out. I can spot operational obstacles, operational roadblocks.

There's a huge amount that vendors can do if they have true SaaS software which not all of them do and I am willing to build the big data infrastructure I need to aggregate those clicks you know swipes, nose touches. By the way dogs can use iPads, I just want to mention that because they do nose swipes. If I collect all of that and I have a proper big data infrastructure for storing it and analyzing it as a vendor I can really benefit tremendously and of course the customer's then benefit because then I'm able to deliver better product. But the other piece of it is with the permission of course of my customers if I can aggregate data, data about the work force, data about salary, data about longevity in positions, data about performance making it anonymous that is independent of what company, what individual and I can aggregate that into benchmarking data again using a big data technology infrastructure and analytical techniques.

Now I have an offering for my customers when that customer's trying to make a hiring decision. I can say to them across our install base of the 27 companies we have that are in your industry with your issues, who are hiring a CIO, this is the profile. I mean that's tremendously beneficial and we do have some vendors in the space who are both, have the right underlying architecture for doing this, who are growing in size where they're large enough to have statistically reliable benchmarking data and it's all done without surveys, you know without all that questionnaire stuff. This is huge. So when we talk about big data there's an end user perspective on it but there's also a vendor perspective on it.

Most definitely Naomi and speaking of vendors we, I know that we had talked in pre-show a little bit about a mentor, a huge, huge, huge icon of the HR technology and just general technology space, passed away this week and I wanted to give you a little bit of, a few minutes we got about five and a half minutes left to chat a little bit about that.

Bryan, the gentleman who passed away was Klaus Tschira, heir Dr. Klaus Tschira. He was one of the five founders of SAP and as a particular interest to us as an industry in the HR space because he was the real champion on that founding team for their getting into what was that of course personnel automation and payroll but he was also because his background is a mathematician and physicist he also had a perspective on data that was very much ahead of his time.

In 1993 I actually published a tutorial it was what they called a critical success but a commercial failure all 800 pages of it in which I espoused and I think it was the first time anybody ever had espoused a formal data model for the human resource management domain, a formal set of architectural principles for automating that domain and frankly I got a lot of pushback. I was considered, you know, "She's bright but she's certainly very academic, not terribly practical." My ideas were given not a whole lot of positive feedback and then Klaus appeared. He had read the book and at IHRIM conference in 1993 when we were selling the book from a booth, really the tutorial because it was two books, he comes with this booming voice that could fill a room, "I must find Naomi. She is a genius." and that's how we met. He really gave me a great deal of encouragement at a time when I needed it.

What's interesting for me is that the products, the software products of that era on which everybody was running had such bad data designs that any real attempt at analytics was going to fail. Not because the analytical tools were bad the underlying data was so screwed up. Anybody who's old enough remembers the employee status code where whatever we didn't know we stuck in there. Actually there's still products today which don't have position and jobs straightened out, don't distinguish properly between the individual in the role they're playing but Klaus was a real thought leader in this area and you know a friend and colleague and a mentor and I will miss him very much and he was only 74. Which may sound old to your readers but I'll be 70 this year and 74 sounds really young.

Naomi, I definitely appreciate you sharing that because those are some of the you know some of the icons because technology is a little bit, I think in general is a fairly, is a newer industry that it's so now becoming such a pervasive, touching everybody, especially with social technology and Apple, it's kind of like put hands on everybody from a consumer perspective. So you know when you start talking about publishing things in 1993 that almost sounds, you're really quoting some history, that's what's interesting because that's not that long ago even for me so but for a lot of people you know if you're a 26 year old programmer or a data scientist when you start talking '93 that's a different time so that's fantastic. Well Naomi thank you so much for coming on. You've probably got time for one more closing thought and then we'll wrap it up and have enjoyed your perspective as usual.

Bryan, thank you. I think in closing, just two quick points. One, we've got the technology we can really do this. Now we have a lot of good work going into the algorithms. They're still embryonic but they will get better. Now the burden is on the HR professional community. They have to do the heavy lifting of figuring out what are they right questions to ask and vetting the algorithms that goes with those questions to make sure for their company it's the right, they're going to get the right answers. They're going to get valuable answers and that means they better know math, they better understand data science. We've moved from art form to more engineering and scientific discipline and very few HR professionals have that in their academic preparation. I think a lot of folks are going back to school. I highly recommend Khan Academy's statistics courses.

Well you heard it here folks. Get back to doing the math; I love that actually love that suggestion. I've actually took an additional algebra and stats class since I've been an adult just to figure out what I didn't figure out when I was younger so. Well Naomi thank you so much I hope you have a great rest of the week and we'll look forward to talking to you and crossing paths here in the near future.

Ivan Casanova, Jibe

Future of Big Data in HR

I would like to introduce Ivan Casanova. He's the SVP of Marketing for Jibe. Ivan welcome to Thug Metrics.

Thanks for having me. I'm a big fan. I love the show. So I'm really excited to be here.

If you would go a little deeper in what you do with Jibe, maybe your background and then let's kick it off after you give us a little more about yourself, what's the biggest surprise in in 2015 from your clients?

Sure Bryan. So I joined Jibe a little less than a year ago. I spent the previous twenty years working in enterprise IT. The thing that's really surprised me this year is the demand for analytics and metrics in the HR technology world. And yet, they really haven't gotten that far. So we work with the customers in the world on enhancing their recruiting strategies, allowing them to do things that they weren't ever able to do before they started working with us as a company. You know, people apply for jobs on their mobile phones, setting up all kinds of new talent networks, enhancing the candidate experience that people have when they come to your career site. All of these things are throwing off all kinds of metrics and all kinds of data, and clients really do want to get their hands around these numbers, our clients have a lot of demand, they want to understand it. I just don't think that they've gotten very far. And that's really been the most surprising thing for me. The difference between how far these folks have actually gotten with big data and how much they really have a demand to understand analytics deeper in their organizations.

Where do you feel the resistance is coming from within the human capital practice?

Yeah. Bryan, I think it's a couple of things. First off, I think that this is a people industry. I think that the people who work in HR and recruiting are people oriented. So maybe the use of analytics is a little foreign to them. I think in general we're going to have to rethink a little bit of the skill set that we hire. How we train our own internal people in the organizations to use this technology, to embrace it, to understand what analytics and data can mean to the day-to-day business, and how they should use data to talk to their managers and talk to the executives in the organization. How they should use data internally amongst their own team.

So really kind of build a culture of data inside of HR organizations, that's going to be big. I just don't think we have that today. And I think a lot of it is a bit of a legacy perspective, again where these folks are people oriented employees. That's one.

The second big piece for me is that we've got to do a better job in breaking down the walls of data that are out there. I spent the last twenty years working in marketing. As a marketer I can look at a single dashboard that has data from my own website, data from Salesforce.com, data from a marketing automation system, and all that data's been mashed up together. It's been put into some kind of a data warehouse. It's been put into some kind of rationalized data perspective. And I can actually look at all that information without having to worry kind of which system it came from. That's pretty much general practice today in most marketing organizations, at least in any kind of a large organization. But yet, a lot of the system vendors have built up walls that make it really hard to get data in and out of the core HR technology systems.

Every year Jibe does a survey of job seekers and HR professionals. Last year's survey was really interesting. The average HR professional is spending eight to ten hours a week just pulling reports. That's a crazy number! Right? Because that means that I'm trying to pull a report from one system, and one system only, and I'm spending that much time trying to do it. So we've got to figure out a way to make the data more accessible to people.

If you make data more accessible to people, I think there's one universal truth out there in the big data ecosystem is, the more data you give people the more they want. So we've got to just make the data a lot more accessible.

And I think the third piece of it also, for me is that us as vendors haven't really done enough to make analytics and big data consumable. What I mean by that is, I think we say we're going to build this great analytics application and we're going to put all these amazing online data analytics, widgets on the screen, and you're going to be able to do all the filtering, and you're going to be able to see all these amazing metrics. Yet, we don't really think about how can we as vendors build analytics applications that make it really easy for a knowledge worker in HR to consume that information.

I'll give you the perfect analogy. Jibe has this awesome custom advisory council where we bring ten or fifteen or our best customers together a couple of times a year. We ask them about the state of the industry. What do they think about the key topics? And the last one that we did, the whole focus of it was on analytics. One of the guys on the council says to me, "Hey Ivan, what do you think is the most pervasive and most broadly used analytics application in the history of man?" It's a big question Bryan, don't you think?

Yeah Ivan, it's a pretty decent size.

[Laughter] So I kind of fumbled for an answer and I didn't really know how to answer it. I made some pretty poor guesses and he said to me, "It's the car dashboard." And I thought about. Think about all the analytics we consume when we're driving a car, how fast we're going, the miles per hour, it's the most pervasive and broadly used analytics application in the history of mankind. And what's so amazing about it is, it is analytics delivered in the context of what we're doing, which is driving a car. How can we do that for HR technology professionals? How can we embed analytics into their software applications? Into the workflows that they do, so they don't have to stop doing what they're doing, and to go an analytics app to try to figure out what's going on. Or they don't have to go to some other application and log in to look at their metrics because their boss asked them a question about a key metric.

So I don't think we've done a good enough job in creating analytics applications that are done in context. That was a pretty long answer to a pretty simple question of why haven't we gotten far enough. I don't we've gotten enough access to the data. I don't think we've trained the people well enough. And I don't think the vendors have created those kind of compelling applications that embed analytics into their daily workflows in a way that makes it really simple to use.

Ivan, I have an interesting concept to throw at you here. Why isn't the human capital valued like every other asset in the company? Even Goodwill, which is literally close to unicorns and rainbows, still values. Why isn't it that your human capital actually has a valuation associated with it relative to the overall value of your company?

Yeah, I just think there's a legacy mindset that treats human capital and human capital management as a cost center Bryan. As we have now turned the corner from a really difficult economy and we start to see a little bit more of a consistent growth pattern across the board in all different types of industries, I think everybody is starting to agree that it's harder and harder to hire people. And it's really harder and harder to hire really good people. So I'm encouraged when I see things like in the annual report to come out like Bersin and Deloitte, where they feel like human capital, recruiting in general, are much higher minded issues for C-level executives than ever before. I see that C-level executives in the clients that we speak to, and the customers that we have, say all the time that recruiting is becoming a much more strategic business issue across the organization. People really care about it a lot more and they're talking about it. I think that's the first step into what you're talking about. Where we can actually now put some real economic numbers around our human capital and start to treat it like the asset that it should be.

I don't think we're there yet. I think everybody would agree. But admitting that this is a really big issue and recruiting is a big deal. And getting the right people in the organization is a big deal. And how much money these organizations are actually spending on this, that's a first good step. But I think with the economy where it is today, and only improving, I think this will only grow in importance inside of the organizations. At least that's what we see. And again, Jibe's view of the world is roughly speaking you can it the Fortune 2000 type of organizations.

Our focus is on the biggest organizations that do the most hiring, who create a large percentage of the growth in our economy, and those are the guys we spend most of our time talking to. And that's what they're telling us, across the board really, keeping the right people in the organization, using metrics to figure out the profiles of the right people to keep in the organization, investing in people, investing in recruiting and investing in the right technology and the right strategies for recruiting, and to get those right kind of folks in the organizations. Those are the key things that are starting to resonate at C-level of the organizations and that's a really good first step I think.

Ivan when we get there it will just improve things because of just the objective nature of kind of where things are working and where things are not. Just process improvement in general. Where do you feel the HR function is actually at least at par with the kind of data game, versus lagging? Is there someplace that's a shining kind of star of the HR life cycle?

Interestingly enough Bryan, I think that HR is doing some interesting investments and some interesting advancements like predictive analytics. It's really one of the areas where HR folks might be slightly ahead. What I mean by that is we're starting to see a whole class of vendors and a whole class of companies who are now saying here's what the best employee in your organization looks like. Because they're the ones doing the best on the review process, and they're the ones who are staying the longest, they're the ones who are being promoted the longest. Creating some kind of profile of what that ideal employee looks like. Now here's where it gets interesting and exciting and where I think the HR folks in general are making some huge strides, we're starting to see those ideal profiles now incorporated into recruiting.

A lot of times we spend, in the recruiting software business that Jibe is in, we spend it thinking about how to get more resumes. How to get more candidates, how to get a higher number of applications for a particular job opening? I think there's always going to be job openings where that's really important, for the volume based hiring. But for more and more perspectives and different types of jobs, it's about the quality. It's about finding the right candidates the fastest. This is why I think we're seeing some really interesting advancements is if I can go through a whole pool of candidates and say these are the best ones, based on predictive analytics, based on a whole bunch of data about which employees have been really successful in my organization. And then translating that into recruiting so that our recruiters aren't focused on saying, hey would this person be a good fit? But knowing that this person fits the profile of somebody who would be an ideal fit for my organization that would be tremendous. And I think it's one of the areas where interestingly enough we've made some advancement that are above and beyond what other parts of the organization are doing.

I think it's a byproduct of a real change in HR that we see coming really quickly, which is — for the last twenty years we've thought that the paradigm for recruiting was job advertisements and with an apply now call to action. And I think we're seeing a bit of a change now. What we're seeing is that larger organizations specifically, are starting to curate their own pools of sourcing. So they're building talent networks. They're aggregating all the data from their app tracking systems or from their talent networks, to build their own pools of candidates. And then applying these types of algorithms to find out which of candidates would be good candidates for particular jobs and then pushing apply now calls to action out to those candidates based on their ranking from the algorithms.

I think that's where we see the future of big data in HR, right there in that organizations building large candidate sourcing pools themselves, keeping all that data as a strategic asset for their business and using algorithms to figure out which of those candidates would be great for particular jobs. And you see the beginnings of that in all different kinds of technologies that are out there. You see that with things like email job alerts, which is something Jibe's been doing for a while. You see that with building of talent networks, something that we've been really invested.

Bryan, all of this is really the evolution of recruiting into marketing. Recruiting has become and is becoming, a specialized form of marketing. And I think the use of big data, the use of analytics, predictive analytics especially, are some of the areas where we're seeing this kind of happen more quickly and have a much larger impact than in other parts of the business. So it's a really exciting time to work in HR. I think that's the amazing thing about it. It's a really, really interesting time to be in this industry. And the kind of customers that we work with and the demand that we see for this stuff, it's crazy what an exciting time it actually is to work in this type of industry.

Where does mobile change the game, Ivan? Or impact the moving forward or the innovation within the HR function?

Yeah Bryan, this is something obviously that Jibe is really well known for and we think it's a complete game changer. I just spent the last week with four teenagers on my vacation. They're glued to their mobile phones, none of them had a computer, and they never use a computer. For them, the Internet is their mobile device. So that was in my face for the last week. But more broadly, if we go back and we look at our own research, we see some amazing things happening as far as mobile job search. 80% of the candidates that we interview say they expect to do some part of their job search on mobile. Eighty percent, that's an amazing number. Half of those people say they should be able to do the entire process on mobile. And we thought that number was really high until we saw some research published by some of the folks who kind of measure this stuff on a regular basis.

So the Pew Research guys who do a really great job in understanding how the people are using the Internet came out with a statistic last year that said a third of the people that they surveyed said that they are mobile Internet only. So that's an amazing stat that I talk about all the time with my clients. Which is a third of your candidate pool only accesses the Internet through a mobile device.

So if you haven't optimized the job search on your career site, the application process, all of the entire end to end process. If you haven't optimized it for mobile, you are cutting off a third of the candidate pool. Because the amazing thing about this is we've gotten to a place with mobile today what people are so well trained to expect an awesome user experience on mobile. I mean we use these apps every single day and the user experience on most of these consumer facing mobile applications is so amazing. It's so detailed. It's so rich. It's so easy to use, so easy to understand. Now we come to expect that. And if you are on your mobile phone, if you're on a tablet, or if you're on a mobile device, and you are looking for a job and you are doing the job search, and it's a crappy experience or it's non-existent because there are some companies today that simply don't support mobile at all.

Bryan, a couple things are going to happen. One is, yeah you're not going to apply for that job. That's an easy and obvious one. But what we're also seeing is it has a residual hangover effect. What I mean by that is the person who is on their mobile device has a really bad experience, they're going to have negative brand images about your organization. They're going to think that your company is backwards. They're going to think that you organization is not technology savvy. They're going to think that your company is not the kind of company I want to work for. I'm going to tell my friends on social media that, because we live in a world where our thoughts and our ideas are always shared over social media. And I probably won't even want to buy stuff from you because why would I want to do business with a backwards organization? So I tell all the clients that we work with. Mobile is your brand. Your brand is on mobile. And mobile is an end-to-end experience. Because the weakest link in that chain is going to be where the candidate is going to opt out and he's going to run. He's not going to walk and because he's going to think negative thoughts about you. And it's actually going to impact your brand and your revenue.

Well those are golden words Ivan. Those are potentially billion dollar words you just shared. And to quote the great Fred Sanford, "Get your mobile squared away you big dummy."

You know, I agree with Bryan. And here's the thing, for the clients that we work with who have optimized their career site, their candidate experience for mobile, we see some pretty unbelievable statistics coming out. One is they're getting half their applications from mobile now. That's an unbelievable statistic. The other unbelievable statistic is this, the average time it takes to complete a job application, if you've optimized the application process for mobile, it actually takes about the same amount of time that it takes on a desktop. So we're seeing half the applications come from mobile, and we're seeing peer performance for both the time and the conversion perspective, happening on mobile. So for the companies doing it writes, the huge opportunity is they've basically created a peer platform to the PC. And that's a big deal.

Absolutely Ivan, it's so obvious of where you can make money with a process improvement. You provided some stats that I think are so compelling, and just you're overall thought process around your recruiting function. If you're just presenting dead ends, which I think a lot of people are because the pathways really don't go anywhere, or they linger so long the drop off is so significant. I mean that is just talent that is walking away very easily, because there are so many options to put your information into a company into a recurring workflow now. I mean that's just the world we live in.

Bryan, I was working with a client the other day. I told them the saddest thing in the world is a web page that says to complete your job application you need to go to a computer. And I said, could you imagine if Amazon, who continually gets more and more of their traffic and ecommerce through mobile devices, said you need to go on a computer? That's the equivalent to what we're telling folks today if you don't have your optimized mobile apply flow, career site, end-to-end process optimized for global. We're doing the equivalent of telling you that you can only buy stuff from a PC.

Ivan, what's your prediction for 2020, where do you put your future as an add-on, real quick.

Sure. I think that going forward the largest organizations are going to lead the way. I think that we are building a generation of data driven recruiters. One of the things that we've done here at Jibe is that we built an online educational site called the Data Driven Recruiter. You can Google it; you can find this on Twitter under the Data Driven Recruiter. What we're doing is, Brian you participated in this and a bunch of other business industry luminaries have participated in this. And what we're doing is we're educating the global recruiting world on the use of analytics in their organizations. I'm a firm believer here that the rising tide will lift all ships. And so my big prediction for out and into the future, and I don't think it's as far out as 2020, is that the majority of the recruiting organizations are using data to govern their decision making process.

They're more effective, they spend less, they're targeting better and their overall recruiting function is going to be way more efficient because the data is coming, and the tools and the vendors are providing those type of solutions that the clients are going to find really affective.

I love seeing what the vendors are presenting year over year, I know 2015 has been interesting and I hope at the end of the year, HR Tech that there's some things that just can start blowing our minds on reimagining the process.

So, we've got about ninety seconds left. I'll let you close it up with a final nugget of wisdom Ivan.

Bryan-Yeah. We're big believers of educating the market, so check out Jibe.com. You can see how good your mobile experience can be there. You can check out the data driven recruiter on Jibe.com. So our website is chock full of educational resources, so I urge everybody to go out there and take a peek, because we really are committed to educating folks in this marketplace. Bryan, it's been a blast. I really enjoyed every minute of it. This is a good way to start my workweek back up after a nice vacation.

David Bernstein, eQuest

Believe in the Data

Welcome to Thug Metrics. This show is all about big data, small data, medium data and data-data-data-data. I want to get to our guest. We're going to have a great little debate conversation today. It will be fun. David Bernstein, welcome to Thug Metrics.

David is the Vice President of the Data Analytics division of eQuest.

David, how would you sum up, what's a good analogy from your lens of big data within the human capital practice?

Well you know Bryan, I speak on this topic quite a bit and in the SHRM world especially, what comes to mind often is it's almost like how folks treat money. They know that they want to grow it, they want to be with it, they want to understand it, and they need so much help with it. It's a challenge. It's not something that comes naturally, and yet it's something that's key to the future.

Those that do well either have a natural gift, and that's maybe those that are inclined to go down a career path that's more relative to this data and analytics and driving numbers into the conversation. Or there are the folks that hopefully seek out the advisorship to help them get a better grip on it. I think that might be a great way to kind of frame it. Then there's those that maybe think that they should be doing something but then don't get around to it. Always knowing in the back of their mind that it's something they should be doing but it somehow managed to slip away.

So David at the core I see you as a behavioral scientist that deals a lot with data. So, lets talk about money, I think about retirement. In theory I think retirement is an interesting thing. I don't plan on really doing it, I just plan on it being a place that I can do whatever I want. That's my version of retirement. But say that I did want to retire at seventy years old, and I know that I need to save X amount of money every single month, every single year to get there. Right? I know that. I'm definitely not the smartest guy in the room, but I'm definitely not last in the class either. But I still probably don't save what I need to get there. I save twenty-five, fifty, seventy-five percent, and a hundred percent a couple months. I know that I have to do that to get where I want to go. We're talking thirty years out, give or take a few years by the way and it's just the pain is not great enough.

Is that really what we're talking about here David? Is the pain isn't great enough, or the threat isn't enough that data becomes a priority and significant within the HR practice?

You know Bryan, that's a great way to kind of segue from all of it. Now that hierarchy of needs often comes to my mind as I'm sitting and talking with teams of HR folks who will lament. Because there's not been an HR crowd yet that isn't interested in this. It's not that they don't want to know or try or incorporate. It's the save-for-college-knowledge that I ought to do that. But the reality that I've got to put food on the table right now, going back to the money picture even. The reality of what's facing much of HR when they're in teams of one to five, a predominant HR grouping, the time in a day it's painful to sit back and know that they ought to be thinking about how to grow this, incorporate this and get access to this. And yet the reality of all the fires and getting payroll right and onboarding people, and all the demands, trying to just be that great alms person for the employees, fill all these recruiting orders, be that advisor to the executive team. Trying to manage all that and also grow a skillset that wasn't necessarily drove and attracted people into HR twenty years ago, as well as it wasn't what was needed. The need of the hour has emerged out of this kind of online competitive, accelerated speed, which is ironically what drives big data as well. The vast connectedness of this allows this data to fly fast and amass it in buckets that are bigger than ever. That's really the essence of this big data.

When you collect all that behavioral data and do the statistical analysis of all this, you can find signals in that pile of noise. That's really the heart of it. And this human behavior that the HR teams sit on top of, that captures those behavioral moments, there's gold in there. But figuring out how to get to it, how to understand it, how to analyze it and make it relative to the businesses that they operate in, on top of just the day to day. I think there you go, right? It might be a long segue from your statement of the pain. They've got to get through their day and they're not being managed to do something other than that, and yet the world around them is highlighting this need and availability. It's a swirl, right?

David, it sounds like to me, data is really a big picture opportunity, but unfortunately it's too strategic. It can't be consumed at this point in time, it appears it hasn't been adopted, and the consumption is really a struggle for your HR practitioner. There's just a gap.

Yes. If I hand you a scalpel Bryan, are you going to be a surgeon? And the amount of work it takes to get to have the precision, the expertise to use that instrument well, there's a lot of steps to get there. And if you can't get there overnight on your own and you need help, then you need help in terms of time and resources and funding. HR certainly needs to make some business case for this. But also the enterprise that they operate in needs to create that opportunity that supports them in getting there. It's a handshake that needs to happen. It's not just a finger wagging moment at HR. Certainly do they need to get more analytic data minded? Sure. They need to push for that. It's ironic; I was talking with one of my friend who manages the analytic team at a large financial company. He was saying his incoming MBA HR folks are all about the data, and they know very little about HR. And on the other side of him are all these kind of tenured HR leaders who know everything there is to know about the business and HR, but they know very little about how to incorporate the data. There's not a happy medium. And so data teams today really have to figure out how to be that. How to get the HR teams to be more data minded and believe the data. And how to school up the incoming business minded HR folks, as they're saying all the tool kits in HR now are really all about analytics. But twenty years ago if you'd said that's what HR's all about? There's really a dichotomy here at the moment and it will be interesting to see how this plays out.

Yeah, as we discussed in pre-show, it's not going away. It's been around a long time David. It's now maybe called some different things. There's access to it. You have different views of it. People are pairing it up with different elements of information. Some of this data, it's been around for a long time. It's only going to get more prevalent in the day-to-day conversation and operation across the whole supply chain David, it's significant. That's the part that I think is interesting. HR has people that touch everything, and so that's why they're kind of getting called and called out on the fact that they don't a lot of times have a handle on how people are touching the organization. They can make an impact relative to measurement and the data intelligence to driving the revenue and the profit of a company.

Completely Bryan. That's why HR should exist, right. There's certainly is a people operations component. They're table stakes at this point. So you want to do the HR for the best cost on that front. But the opportunity to understand how to take people and drive that to what the company's goal and mission is. That's really the opportunity here. There are so many underlying activities to get to that. Just even simple data governance and data cleansing, organization and business processes that go with that. There's a fair amount of steps that it's going to take. You can't just do analytics, even if you wanted to, on top of data that is horribly amassed. You'll get horrible results. It's almost worse to do that than to do nothing. You know? Making decisions or trying to predict behavior off of information that's either the wrong information in it, the wrong business cycle, it can lead to some really ugly activity.

I mean I've spent most of my activity in the shop here pulling all that together. That's really I think the opportunity even now on the vendor side, is to really come with these tailor made capabilities and not come to market with solutions that expect someone else to go do all that heavy lifting. But to really organize that at this stage, that's the market opportunity at this point. Selling dashboards and expecting all the data to suddenly materialize. Anyway, I'll go down that path some other time maybe on the tech show. [Laughter]

Bottom line is, there's a lot of work involved and somehow it's got to get done. And maybe there's a group of smart people on the vendor's side, maybe it's the internal world, but also the enterprise leadership needs to also create that need and the demand for that, and the appetite for that. And understand that the cultural shift includes them in making that happen.

Are there any good examples that off the top of your head you can share around data that is so compelling that it would make a practitioner within the practice of a company, want to dig in where they stand against that stat?

Bryan, that's what we try to bring is a fair amount of external information and blend it up with what's going on for the employer Bryan. So that they can make better sense of their recruitment and marketing efforts and is it producing and are there other opportunities and how is it that the wisdom of the crowd and how do you blend that with trends and macroeconomic situations with unemployment rates for example, and supply and demand? When they're doing the recruiting, obviously that's not a spectator sport. That's a full court press activity because they've decided they can't live without filling that position. Right? You'd think that they'd want to be able to do that with excellence and speed. On the HR front, that's I think the pieces. You know, understanding that there is data out there and whether you're going to find it in your buckets or you're going to go seek it out.

It's the incumbent activity I think right now, the paramount activity may be a better word, and for the HR team right now is to want to be data minded. Maybe that's kind of the spark that they need to get lit, the little spark under them right now needs to be let's go. And there is so much pressure out there. So let's not ignore it. Yes we know we need to save for college and we're trying to put food on the table, but let's not just say it's thirty years out. The need of the hour is now. This information and the speed of which business is moving is too quick. It's hard to imagine.

The other low hanging fruit areas where HR has quick access to information certainly on the selection world, has been doing this for a real long time. They've been using large datasets to try to figure out who are going to be the better fits for your company coming in. And there's a whole lot of work going on right now about trying to look at what are the indicators in the data that telegraph people are looking to leave. And in those situations, when they're part of your vital few, how do you kind of see that signal ahead of the cycle, right? It's all about trying to narrow cast in and try to find key patterns that you either want to mitigate or to leverage, is really where it bottoms out.

David, is there any exciting tools you've recently that you've seen that you find kind of what the future looks like? As you're analyzing data, capturing data, marrying data, anything that you wanted to share with us? Not endorse, we're just talking about it, for the record.

Well, yes certainly. My role provides me the access to experiment let's say, with a fair amount of the technology out there. In my previous roles as an internal HR technology leader in corporate enterprise settings, I can compare what I'm looking at today to what I used to be faced with on the buy side. The order of magnitude and the pricing are incredibly different as well the power of these tools. What I've been looking at are tools that are not really on the dash-boarding side, which is where I know a lot of the attention is. That's kind of easy. Certainly telling stories with the data, that's a critical component and moving from dashboards into pictures of the data.

Heat maps, for example, are great ways to understand. One friend of mine, she was telling me how they actually figured out how to change there staffing plan, their improvement plan, based on their attrition data. When they plotted it on a heat map Brian, they were looking at the leave rates and they stumbled upon zip code, because they could see the heat, the intensity of the leaving relative to these zip codes. And when they dug deeper into that they found it was relative to their business relies on the hourly population, who for the most part in that city where they were experiencing the largest attrition didn't have access to a car, relied on public transportation. And those zip codes were poorly served by public transportation. Clearer, analyzed the data visually.

I would certainly endorse any kind of tool set that really takes it beyond red lights and green lights, into kind of letting you understand where your pockets of things are happening. I've also been looking at data science tools that actually incorporate the fancy analytics. And your job isn't to necessarily know SaaS or R or any of these other data analytic packages, but to know how to bring the right data to bear, and then feed it through these mechanisms. You know, the predictive analytics and a cloud based service tool where you can upload your data in and the pictures will emerge, as long as you're bringing the right datasets together.

Bryan, it's the smartness on knowing what data, and then how to understand what the pictures are telling you relative to the business context of that data. That's where the great opportunity is on the HR front right now. They don't have to become expert in the data science.

That's the part David, I don't know if it just starts to get overwhelming for folks. When it's dramatically outside your competency area and you just don't know where to start, and you probably are a little under resourced. So it's an extra thing. Yes, it's somewhere on our priority list, but it just doesn't happen to hit the top of the fold any day. You might go to a lunch or you might get an hour or you might have a great conversation, but the actual execution of how does it incorporate into the day, much less a strategy. I think that's the part where people just kind of – and we have some differing opinions on this – but I think people kind of just give up. It's like, you know what? I'm just going to tackle what I can to make damn sure that I keep my job. And that ends up being all right with a lot of executive teams, because they're running the business.

My cynical side says that the people organization still is not a priority. If it was a priority, they would hire somebody or they would make some-body, the dedicated data person within the human capital or HR practice, at every single company. To figure out how they can leverage those assets that are sitting there that actually can be grown internally. It just perplexes me that it just doesn't become a priority.

So where's the tipping point, Bryan? Where is this? Where's the watchful eye in HR that's saying, from a professional organization, beyond just any one company. The SHRMs of the world and the national agendas on this, sure it's perplexing. But there's got to be a tipping point. There are growing numbers of stories, maybe I'll live on Walden Pond a bit and be kind of hopeful and see the greater good. You know, I'll go back to if we can get an HR profession to understand the opportunities, great. It's easier to access. It's much more affordable. And start thinking about this whole idea of the need to find the cost effective, easy ways to start dipping my toe in the pond, then I think we've got an opportunity to get a crack in the dome. Otherwise, is HR going to be relegated back to the place where they've long not wanted to be, which is just wanting to be that kind of operational group. We talked earlier about the strategy behind this. This is what fuels the ability to be strategic. It's the "I know" versus "I think" oriented statements. Here's the data, here's what I know that's happening, here's what I can say I'd recommend now. Blending that part in a science. But yeah, I'm going to be hopeful. I'm still going to go out on the road and push and advocate for this. Sitting all day with talent acquisition teams trying to convince them that there's a better way. So you know, it's daunting; it's a knife fight in the jungle at times.

Well is it running kind of a parallel life cycle or I guess more of a reference similar life cycle, as incorporating or adopting technology into recruiting? Recruiting seems to be a little bit more leading edge, just in the sense that it's a pretty cheap entry point, relative to getting a recruiting system, like HRIS. Having things touching like the rest of beyond recruiting, onboarding on. A little bigger because it touches all of operations, it touches all of finance, it touches everything. And so that takes a lot more to get done. Do you parallel this to – it took a long time to get people on board that they needed a system, something to manage all that information, versus doing everything in QuickBooks and Excel. Is it kind of running a similar kind of maturity life cycle?

Bryan, I guess I see what you're saying. Sure. But the timelines that go with those cycles are definitely different than they've ever been. I guess that's the sense of urgency that drives us. I'll go back to what's created the opportunity, whether you call it big data or not, it doesn't have to be Wal-Mart size information, the speed of Google. The opportunity to have connected data flowing is a much different pace and the costs to get that connectivity today is driven down so much, that that's why this data is flowing into collected ponds. If HR doesn't understand that that's happening all around them, enterprises are about business function. You know John Boudreau talks about this, he's been trying to advocate for analytics for twenty years. He and Lawler at the Center of Organizations, they've been trying to move this needle for a long time. Boudreau's book on Retooling HR is all about leveraging the business models with the frameworks of data analytics that supply chain, marketing and sales have long had.

It's lifting and shifting those and bringing those into the HR context, but not having to reinvent, so that HR can leapfrog and jump into this quicker. There are a lot of us on the sidelines, trying to corral the troops. The need of the hour is for the HR world to kind of grapple with where we started the whole conversation. Do I save for college or do I buy food for now? Is it really that kind of binary moment? It's really not. It's about trying to figure out how you do both. My energy in the conversation is getting folks to find ways, small ways, to get into big data.

Well, David I think there's an opportunity for you to be Suze Orman of big data. How about that? We can productize that up and get you a talk show. You've got a face for TV; you're a good-looking guy. I think we've got this solved. I feel pretty good about that suggestion by the way, as you can tell. I hate to always ask about version one, but once you have an understanding of it, and a willingness, which is a big part, what's version two of big data? Or what's the second step to be more of a data driven organization?

Bryan, believing the data; I mean you've got to get it and then believe in it. You're always testing the veracity. And they say in big data that the volume, variety and velocity but the fourth "V" often referred to is veracity. And if you get the truth into the data, but then when you've done all that work, have some belief in it. Leverage that; blend that with what you know about what's going on in the organization and about the business. I'll go back to art and science, but bring that data into the conversation and start to get comfortable and practice it. People will respect you. You'll greatly increase the reputation. It's not an opinion and it's not limited to your personal experiences. So yeah, have some belief in the data and start practicing using it in your conversations.

Damon Cortesi, Simply Measured

You Can Never Have Too Much Data

Welcome Damon Cortesi to Thug Metrics.

Damon is one of the co-founders of Simply Measured, one of my favorite, and possibly the best social media analytics tool on the freaking planet. So I feel great that we're able to get a few minutes with you. So kind of jumping into it, tell us a little bit what the path was that got you and what was the cocktail napkin or the genesis for Simply Measured getting started? Because I'm sure where it started, the idea stage to where it is today, is maybe so different than you ever thought it would be that sometimes you pause and you go wow, it's hard to believe we've went that far. So share some thoughts on that real quickly.

Yes, certainly. I'll share a couple of things. One, to the point you say wow I didn't even realize we would get here. We actually first started as a company, our name was called Untitled Startup Incorporated, that was our legal entity. We didn't know exactly what we were doing, like must startups five years ago. We didn't have a product or a business plan. We just knew we wanted to do something in social. And we eventually got around back to social analytics. I got into that around 2007 or so, that's when Twitter was starting to become pretty popular among the nerds and geeks out there.

I was actually traveling abroad and I was about to hit my two-thousandth tweet, which doesn't sound like a lot today, I have about fifty thousand plus today. But I was really curious whom the heck I was talking to and why I was tweeting so much, why was I using this platform with a bird and a fail whale selection?

I think it literally was a cocktail napkin. Like I said, I was traveling abroad and I would go out to eat a lot. And I sat down and I started drawing charts of what might be useful metrics to try to analyze myself. I went back to my hotel and I sat down, and like you did in the old days I wrote a little Perl script that actually scrapes my tweets from Twitter.com. Downloaded them into a CSV file and spit out some interesting analytics about who I was talking to, who I was retweeting, what times a day I was talking, all this kind of stuff that's still pretty core to what we do today as a social analytics platform. I built that little Perl script, people downloaded it and seemed to love it. So then I took the weekend, learned Derby on Rails and developed the first Twitter analytics platform called Tweet Stats. And I released that in January 2008 and it's kind of been a rollercoaster since then.

Damon, anytime you can pull out and share about writing a Perl script that is so Smithsonian-like history in this day and age. So you guys didn't go raise a billion dollar funding round, you weren't like a quiet unicorn, which is oddly a little passé in 2015, but still billion-dollar at least sounds cool. So that's not how you guys did it. You literally just started rocking with something that was a pain point and built from there.

Thinking back from that point of you just wanted to see what the true analytics were of the social conversations, what's a surprise looking backing that maybe you got validation or maybe it was a discovery?

Bryan, I'm going to take a little bit of an engineer centric approach on this. And simply one of the surprises to me is that people actually wanted this data. That was something for me that kind of blew my mind. And as we were in the early days of developing products for the

Simply Measured platform, we kept putting out these different products to kind of test the waters. The first one gathered tweets and put them into a Google spreadsheet. And it's a super, super simple concept but people started signing up and people started giving us money. That was actually a huge surprise for little old me, who was just an engineer trying to make something useful that people might want to pick up and use.

And I was just so surprised that they would want to buy that solution. It was just kind of mind bending for me. That's part of the reason that a few months into the company we brought in a third co-founder to actually help build the business. Because we were just a couple of product guys just out they're having fun building products. And we realized that we could actually make a little bit of money off of this, and then we realized we could actually make a pretty big company off of this. It's still very true today.

Companies are spending millions and millions of dollars on advertising and they're still trying to figure out exactly what the benefit of all of that is. And all of the social platforms are really just developing their ad platforms in addition to their native publishing platform, and it's a really, really interesting point in time just because they're growing up. They're public companies right and they really have to justify who they are and where all that spend goes. That was one of the things that were super interesting to me. Here's a little data stream, you know, I scraped some tweets off the Twitter.com website and wow it's actually useful. It's actually valid insights into what's going on the platform. That was always a lot of fun for me to try to dig in and find those insights as well.

Damon, when you wake up in a cold sweat at night and you think God, what's the definition of big data? Because I'm sure that happens all the time, right?

[Laughter] Bryan, yes all the time.

What's your definition when you hear the term "big data"?

I take a very practical approach, Bryan, to it and I see there are two components. One it's the- ingest and the end processing of a large number of data points. Then two, it's the processing of such data at scale. And by that I mean basically anything you can't fit into an Excel spreadsheet. [Laughter] That's really how I think about it. And even that's changing with all the technologies that Microsoft is coming out with for Excel, like Power BI. That's kind of the basic definition to me. You know, anything you can't really sit there on your laptop and figure out how to process.

Excellent. So your organization has been very focused on consumption and what people do with that information once it's been consumed. Two parts to the question: How do you use data on a daily basis in your life, maybe professionally or personally? And how do your clients use data?

So let's start with the how do I use data. And that's always a fun one. I've always been interested in data gathering and visualization. It was one of those things I would do for fun, like I said I built tweet stats back in the day because I was kind of bored in a foreign country. I sat down on a Friday night and scrapped some data from Twitter.com. So these days I'm always kind of keeping an eye out for new networks and things like that.

When Meerkat came out I kind of looked at the API and figured out how to get data out of the API. Strangely one of my favorite things is to send people spreadsheets of data that they didn't realize they could get.

Nice. [Laughter]

That's one of my favorite things to do with our own marketing department, just send them a quick little email. Oh hey, I found out I could get the number of views of every single Meerkat video the past day. Just kind of let them have fun with it. There are a number of other random things that I do too. For example, I'm very interested in how data can make our lives better. So I drive the same route to work every single day and I know there are certain times I can leave or can't leave that may be better for me. And so, one of the things I did was I stood up an Amazon EC2 instance and set it up to get Bing traffic data every five minutes, and tried to figure out what the most optimal route was for me to take into work at any given point in the day. These are some of the things that I do for fun. When I'm bored and I have some spare time on the weekends, which I think says a little bit to my own personality and social network. [Laughter]

Dude, that's awesome.

Little bit of a dork in that sense. And then moving on to how we at Simply Measured do data, a lot of what we do obviously is very data driven. Like I said, one of the big parts of big data is simply ingest and the processing of all of those data points. And that is probably where we spend most of our time. A lot of our customers do have significant datasets, but a lot of them they're looking at their own channel or their own profile. It's really in the tens of thousands of data points, not necessarily in the millions or billions. That's fairly easy to deal with. But for us, getting all of that data is a huge challenge. So I think we have about forty terabytes of data in our database cluster, which isn't a huge amount by any stretch of the imagination. But in order to get that in, we hit a number of APIs throughout the day. A simple example is the Facebook and Instagram API. I think we hit their systems at least four to eight million times a day, so we can try to pull in as much data as we possibly can.

Wow! [Laughter]! That kind of blows my mind a little bit. You know, I'm thinking a few thousand then four to eight million times a day, which makes sense. I mean it's almost like a heartbeat, right? You're hitting that heartbeat, like every time it happens you're trying to hit that because there's new data, that transaction is happening and it never stops, hopefully.

Yeah exactly Bryan, one of the things I pride myself on, and our company on, is that we are very aggressive about making sure we have the most data possible for our customers. That's one thing I love. We're a little bit over-aggressive in hitting those APIs probably. But in the long run it's more beneficial for our customers and they get the best picture possible of what's out there. I love that we're so aggressive about making sure we have as much of that as possible.

And the beauty is the price of storage has dropped so significantly Damon. You can curate a mountain full of data and then come back to it when you need it. So that's awesome.

Bryan, I think that's one of the ways things are going. It's so cheap now, even different than five years ago, to just store that data. You pull it in, you let it sit there, and then there's all these systems that are making it really, really easy to actually query that data at scale.

So we're going to come back, of course, to what the future of data and looking at conversations a little bit later. What's been the biggest, I guess, realization as you help your clients? Because ultimately you guys use it internally, of course to build your business, but you have tens of thousands, if not hundreds of thousands of clients using it to help understand, drive, and enhance the conversation around their brand. Anything that stands out that possibly shocks you that the clients have come back to you and shared?

That's a really interesting question. Trying to think about it off the top of my head. I think one of the things that do shock me is that there's so many different metrics that you can actually measure from all of these different social channels. And when you look at our different reports – I think we have between thirty or forty different stock reports, which are not counting all the customization we do for customers. When you look at that, you have this giant chart, or this giant report, and we're trying to tell a story throughout this entire report. And there's so many different ways to slice and dice the data.

What's still happening in the marketplace right now is there's really not a standard way to look at all of that data. So from that perspective we try to define some standard metrics in terms of engagement and things like. It's really difficult to actually do, and we have all these disparate systems. So let's say somebody's looking at a Facebook report on our system, they have numbers on our system where we collected the data and crunched some numbers. They they'll look at Facebook and there's some different numbers on Facebook. And then they look at Facebook insights and there's some different numbers there. So trying to correlate and collect all these different numbers across all these different systems and make sure that they all matchup is also ridiculously challenging.

That's always one of the things that surprises me, how much there is to measure and trying to figure out what action you took that actually impacted your engagement or impacted your audience, and things like that. You can track that pretty easily. But it's amazing being able to kind of do that A / B testing and looking at it and say, ok we put out this campaign, we used this type of post content, whether it's a video or picture. And it had this impact on our engagement or our audience. It's really, really interesting being able to tie those dots together.

And of course we want to keep going further down that line and say, ok had this impact on engagement, grew our audience by this much, and it resulted in X number of dollars of sales. And that's something we're very close to having that social ROI piece in there. Some places can do it, but it's kind of a method, like a certain place that companies have to be in to have all that data in the right place. Another thing that surprises me as well is simply being able to have all of these systems in place to be able to query them such that you can get a complete picture in one place of everything that's going on. We're not quite there yet, there's still a lot of work.

Damon, like you were talking about the classic ROI. That's ultimately the Holy Grail is being able to point, especially from a marketing stand point, advertising, marketing, running campaigns. Is that really translating all the way down to profitability? Right? That literally is the Holy Grail that people have been chasing forever. And then you throw social on top of it, where you're able to then actually put some metrics because it's using applications to have conversations. It's not literally standing with a clipboard outside a mall entrance, trying to ask people what's going on. So I think it's cool. It's cool you guys are almost there. That's encouraging.

Yeah. And I think the interesting thing too, and one of the surprising things, if you look at a lot of businesses, how many of them are actually run off of Excel spreadsheets? It's a little bit crazy when you start to look at it. We've done some prototyping work with a few different companies where they'll come in and they'll send us an Excel spreadsheet and it will have tabs for all of their social data. Then it will have that last tab that is "spend based on conversions from social" and they're tracking all of this manually. Into some respects that's a little bit terrifying, I can only imagine what that person's job is like that has to maintain that. Oh yeah, yeah, we're huge fans. I think we have about a third of our conference rooms named after Excel functions.

[Laughter] That is awesome! Damon, what's the future of functionality within big data?

Future of functionality: like I said earlier, big data is about two parts. One is just kind of getting all of that little data into one place to make it big. Then the other part of it is processing on top of that data as scale. That second part is becoming really commoditized, especially in terms of the functionality that we have to do calculations over big data. You know, five years ago if you wanted to do this big data thing, you had to stand up an H-base cluster, or HDFS, and learn how to map reduce, and the tools for that were very limited. And you had to be an engineer to be able to do that basically. But now we've got all this great new technology that has really been maturing in the past five years.

You look at Google Big Query and Amazon Red Shift, even vendor products you can download and still install yourself, like Elastic Search. All of a sudden you can make queries over millions and billions of rows of a dataset in a matter of seconds. It's really, really scary how well it works. And you don't really need a ton of engineering expertise. If you want to use Red Shift or Big Query, it's literally just sequel queries. And you can do a select count start or a select sum star and it becomes really, really accessible if you want to try to do any sort of calculation. I like to think that a lot of the advanced analytics out there is really just counting. Right? You're counting things up; you're dividing them by other things. You're not really doing anything too complicated. There are of course some systems where you're actually doing analysis and trying to identify correlations between datasets and things like that. But a lot of analytics out there is literally just counting things, and it's become much easier to count them at scale now. So that's one of the things that I think has become a lot easier, especially in the past several years. It's just so much more approachable to actually be able to do queries over that size of data.

So what's the future of data science, Damon?

Well Bryan, it's a big thing now. I mean you can't find enough of them. And it used to be accountants because nobody wanted to deal with that. They kind of closed the gap a little bit. A lot of us have taken accounting classes, lots of them, and that's more of a possibility. But being a data scientist that is a whole different ball game. That doesn't happen quickly.

No, no it doesn't.

Again, I think we make it a little bit more complex than it needs to be. But at the end of the day, a lot of data science is trying to dig into the data and trying to tell a story through the use of data and calculations. That's a lot of what it is. If you look at some of the data scientist logs out there that I've taken a look at, a lot of what they're doing is, ok we've got this massive dataset. What's interesting about it? That's where I started too. I find it really humorous when I built Tweet Stats back in 2008; people started throwing the term "data scientist" around and analytics around. And I would actually go back to them and be like, it's not really anything too complicated. I mean literally, just storing data in a database and writing sequel queries. But I think exposing that information in a scientific way – if you just look at the roots of the word Data Scientist, it's somebody that has a hypothesis about data and is trying to prove it. Once you prove it you can tell a story about that data. I think the thing about it, to repeat, is just becoming easier and easier to get in there and actually try to find those insights. I think it was really limited. When I started doing it, like I said, I was writing these Perl scripts, I was downloading all this data into CSVs.

I remember working with Gantt chart, way back in the early days. They were a data provider and they had a ton of data and I was able to partner with them to help do insights into the data. I guess I could consider myself a data scientist, but really I was just a hacker who was able to grasp through some files and count things in a unique way. [Laughter] So I have a little bit of trouble seeing the future of that. It's definitely a huge field, but the tools are becoming so much more approachable that is becoming really interesting what's coming out of it.

Let's put the big futurism hat on now. We'll get into the big question. So five years from now, how is this data conversation going to change around, like social analytics?

So social analytics specifically, one of the interesting things we're seeing as a trend is again, the commoditizing of analytics for each social platform. About six days ago, Facebook shut down their search API so you can no longer search for public status posts from the Facebook network. Granted, they kind of replaced that with a platform from datasets where you can actually get information from a number of different posts. But again, for privacy reasons they're not exposing any of that data, they're just exposing the analytics on top of that data. That's something we're seeing more and more often with these mature social networks where they're doing a large number of the analytics themselves, and not so much providing the data that they used to. Which is an interesting trend.

Facebook has their Insights platform. Twitter recently updated their analytics platform. And we're seeing this a lot where the social networks are trying to control the data and the message around it more so than they used to. Twitter is still unique in that you can get nearly every single tweet that comes out of their platform, but that's also changing a little bit. It's a little bit more difficult to work with that. There are a few more restrictions than there used to be around pulling that data and doing interesting things from it.

So from a social analytics perspective that's one of the interesting things I see, that trend of platforms trying to control their own data and their own analytics. And to be honest I'm really happy about that because then it gives you an authoritative source for a number of the different metrics. And the challenge at the end of the day is still acquisition across all of those different platforms. That's one of the things that we are really good about is actually going out to all of these different platforms and gathering this disparate data, and bringing it together in a way that actually makes sense for our customers, and allows them to gain some useful insight based on that data. Extending that to the quote un-quote "big data" industry at large I think the challenge is still data acquisition. There's just so many disparate data sources and we're creating so much more data, there's still not an easy way to bring that all to one place. Think about a smart home, you've got all of these sensors around, you've got all this information. But if you actually want go get access to that right now, if you want to put it somewhere where you can query it, it's not easy. If you want to have some more personalization, like I said earlier I drive to work the same route every single day and I still have to stand up an EC2 instance to try to figure out the best data driven way to work.

But I'm kind of a unique individual in that aspect. [Laughter] But that's the thing, that acquisition is still really difficult. And the personalization of that data and big data is going to become more and more important as those things around. But of course as we move into that realm we have to worry about privacy and all of those fun aspects of it.

So it's going to be an interesting world.

Absolutely. So last question. We've got about thirty seconds left. So what's one thing that like your smaller businesses could do right now to start helping themselves in looking at their social conversations?

So for the smaller businesses that want to try to help further them it's really just get out there and engage with your customers. One of my favorite small businesses is the local brewery in Ballard. They've got a great social presence. They're engaging with their customers. They're getting out there. They're helping draw people into their business just by being loud and getting some influencers and helping spread the word about their business. As a small business, you don't really need measure too much to start off with, you just need to get out there and engage with folks.

Jason Lauritsen, Quantum Workplace

Getting on the Same Page

Welcome to Thug Metrics. Jason Lauritsen welcome to Thug Metrics.

It's good to be here. I don't get associated with the word thug nearly often enough these days. I appreciate you having me here.

Yeah Jason, you know what? You probably do, but we just don't tell you about it. [Laughter]

Fair. That's Fair.

Jason is with an amazing organization out of Omaha, Nebraska. It's Quantum Workplace. He's the Director of Best Places to Work. You guys are really about as data driven of an organization as you possibly can get, and you convey how to be more of a data driven organization to all the clients that you work with. If you could, tell us a little bit about Quantum Workplace and then we'll jump to talking about the whole data conversation after that.

Sure Bryan. Well the marketing version of what we do is that we build tools that help leaders in organizations to make-work awesome for employees. Specifically, our tools are essentially a way to capture and harness the power of employee voice. Capturing employee opinion, employee sentiment about the workplace, and like you said, to make more informed, data driven decisions to reveal insights that help you improve the work place to make things better. So our biggest product is employee engagement surveys, which we use both directly with organizations and to drive our Best Places to Work programs. And then we've also been expanding into the area of applying some innovative approaches to making exit interview data actually usable and actionable as well some performance and recognition platforms as well. So that's the short version, we build tools that help make the workplace better for the employee, in a way that drives better performance.

Excellent. Jason what's your response, when you hear the term "big data"?

You know Bryan; I have mixed reaction to it. Because when I hear that phrase there's sort of two sides of me. One is I love the promise of big data. Like it excites me, it's potential. Especially in the world of HR. There's so much data and so much opportunity in the data that we have access to, if we could figure out how to harness it. So on the one hand it represents promise and optimism and potential for me. But on the other hand, I think big data has kind of taken on almost buzzword status it seems. I think a lot of people when they use the phrase big data; it's just a deflection. They don't really know what they mean I think. It's like we have a lot of data points, we have a lot of stuff, and so we're going to call it big data. And we talk about it as if we know what we're talking about, or as if it's useful. I think it's gotten to be to where it's just getting thrown around a lot and they think that's distracting some people from what the potential is and what we really should be working on.

You bring up a good point Jason. What's a good framework to start thinking about the data conversation? You offer a perspective of an HR practitioner, which you were one in your past life. Here's the setup, you're one of maybe two to four people in an HR organization within a company, and you know that measuring is important. That is kind of like the table stakes of HR typically, as you're looking at the usual suspects, turnover percentages, how quickly you post a job to fill, time to fill ratios, all those things. There are a handful of maybe ten things that you're kind of looking at anyway, that you're getting measured on for performance. So what's a little bit further in thinking, ok how do we become more of a data driven organization outside of what we already sort of measure and report on?

Yeah Bryan. I think this is still the struggle today, is finding connecting points that can connect the data that we have readily available, or that we tend to look at in HR. So the things you just mentioned but the connecting points that connect that to business outcome data, or business indicator or predictor data, that the organization looks at to manage the business. I think one of the lucky things that happened to me in my career was my first HR job; it was with about a thousand-person company out of Omaha that was in a debt collection business. It was largely a call center business. Essentially we were in the call center business. And in the call center business, if you're working at it you can find very direct connection between what you do in HR, sort of these HR metrics, and the actual business outcomes that happen.

So like when we talked about turnover and the cost of turnover, I could give you very specific, real, hard cost implications of what it costs to have a position open for a certain period of time. Or what it would cost if someone was here for a certain period of time and then left. Or what the actual ramp time and what retention actually meant in terms of hard business dollars. That is where I learned to think about that these HR metrics only have meaning when we can connect them to the business outcomes, the things that actually keep our business in business. And so in a call center it's fairly straightforward.

I think it gets harder when you move to other businesses where it's not as obvious or it's not as direct. So I think for most HR people the challenge is figuring out where that connecting point is. Where is there a real connecting point? And if there's not a connecting point, how do I start thinking about creating one? For example, one of the things I've been thinking about lately is Net Promoter Score. Net Promoter Score is one of those things that's a fairly common, and if you're an HR pro and you're listening to this and don't know what Net Promoter Score is, go look at the Wikipedia page and read up on it. That's a good place to start. But Net Promoter is a measure that marketers have been using for years to gauge customer sentiment about their business and about their experience. Would they refer? Would they recommend? That's sort of an accepted kind of standard for a lot of companies on the marketing and sales side.

So one of the things I'm curious about is what if could, or we did, measure Net Promoter Score with employees. And then we could use that Net Promoter as a connecting point directly between employee sentiment and customer sentiment. And we can show that those things sort of move together and are statistically linked.

In our business, now all of a sudden I have an argument to say well here's yet another place where we can see that when engagement goes up, we can actually follow that trail to customer sentiment, customer experience, or customer retention going up, or whatever it is. But that's a situation where you can actually create a linkage. So I think it's really about, as the HR pro, how do you either find or create the linkage between the data you have and that we look at in HR, and the data that the business is run on?

Two parts to this question Lauritsen: how does the size of the organization affect you tackling the data conversation? Let's just call it big data for our thirty minutes we get together today. And also, how does it affect engagement? So you order how you want to answer the questions.

Wempen, the reality on data, the full big data thing, and the bigger the organization is the more likely it is that you have more data. And the more likely it is that you have better technology connected to the data that you have. The downside is that the data complexity is much bigger than it is in smaller organizations. Whereas in a smaller organization you might have to start with how do I collect this data, or how do we capture it in a way that would be easier to analyze. But I think the mistake we make, at least my experience has been, the mistakes you make with the big organization is you try to boil the ocean.

You know, we want to go big data right away. As opposed to saying how about I start with a single department or a single area or a single business unit, and we start looking at just a couple of variables that we have a hunch are the linked ones. Then start there. And if you can make it work in a small group then you can expand and add and make it more complicated. But start as simple as you can. So from a data perspective, that's been my experience. But there are a lot of people that know a lot more about that than I do. As far as engagement, when you asked what the difference is, do you mean the difference in terms of actual engagement level or the difference in measuring engagement? Or working with engagement? Tell me a little more.

Jason it's probably more focused on like engagement level. Like bigger companies, more engaged. I mean, who has an advantage, or is there an advantage?

As far as we've been looking at the trends Bryan, every year we do a sort of a macro-data analysis of all of the Best Places to Work data that we collect throughout the year. Which ends up being data from employees, this year is around six thousand companies across the U.S. So it's a huge dataset. And we break it down in a variety of different ways. But one of the things that is consistent is that engagement is always highest in smaller companies. And when you draw the line out, if I chart engagement level by company size, it goes from really high in the smallest organizations and it drops off, as the organization gets bigger. Engagement it turns out is hard to scale. Which I think some people would find counter-intuitive because the big organizations are viewed as having the most resources, they have the best benefits and they can pay more and all those sorts of things and yet our data shows, year after year that that the small companies are the ones where engagement is always the highest. So it's really fascinating. But when it comes to engagement, small companies definitely have a distinct advantage.

It's interesting Jason, because I think you're exactly right. Relative to when people think about it, they think man I wish I had the resources that the person down the road who has nine thousand employees, they've got so much to throw at awards, recognition and compensation and opportunity and all those things. Is it because we're still trying to figure out the best way to actually address engagement? Why is it such a mystery to this point in time? I mean this is what you guys do, so I think it's fair to ask you this big question. Because we've been doing this for a long time, they've probably been measuring elements of engagement since the 50s. You know what I mean? Really just kind of putting a framework around it, since big company consulting started and people have been trying to figure this out. So are we still missing the mark? We don't have it figured out. Is it technology? What are your thoughts?

Bryan, I think very simply it's been because for the last seventy or eighty years, we have been designing organizations for efficiency, not engagement. It is sort of like for years having a nice culture or all of these things – it just wasn't forefront. I mean what was really driving our decisions about management and about how we ran our organizations was we need to get more efficient. We need to be able to produce a better quality product at a lower cost. So we were squeezing the organization. And the bigger you get, the more pressure there is to produce that sort of optimal efficiency.

So I think what's happened is largely over the years we've sort of squeezed out a lot of the things, or we've lost the ability to do well a lot of the things that we know drive engagement. And this is going to over simplify it, but you take the data points towards what people kind of consider the soft humanistic side of the organization. Things like I want to feel a better sense of connection with the people that I work with. When I feel really connected with the people I work with, I'm more likely to be engaged and to go above and beyond. When I feel valued, appreciated, and recognized, and acknowledged, and seen at work. When I feel respected and trusted. All of those things are the things that at least we continue to find. You know, you keep digging in, like this stuff really is what makes the biggest difference. We have not been designing our organizations to maximize on those things. And that's been a cycle like forever. It's only been probably in the last ten years, maybe fifteen, that we've even been paying that much attention to it.

I feel what happens is that in small organizations you get the entrepreneurs and I think the reality is that in a small organization; it's almost by accident. In some cases it's easier to do some of that because the owner of the company, the president of the company, with their fifteen or twenty or fifty people, like they know each other, they're in it together. Just the nature of the beast makes it feels more connected. And it makes it feel like there's a sense of bond. The other thing we see frequently is that small organizations just invest a lot more time in spending time together. They make room for socializing, not working but being together with their coworkers. We see that frequently in smaller organizations. You don't see as much of that in larger organizations. So there's a lot of stuff that small companies do naturally that has a huge impact on engagement, that large companies have stopped doing. We've sort of engineered a lot of that stuff out of our workplaces, because it looks inefficient.

Sure. So like the people side of things, we're still in the industrial age. I mean the turn of the century type. It's totally Henry Ford. We're still operating under, and I think what you said is so important. To reiterate, designing for efficiency versus designing for engagement is so dramatically different. I mean Apple basically tore that apart. Apple is used as the example relative to design because I think people probably looked at it originally and said this is idiotic, this will never work. But what they were doing is they did the design and then they made the engineering work. I think that's the part that is fascinating. It was a big risk obviously. You had to have this really, very kind of stubborn, driven, resilient leader to get that done. Who got the vision and executed and then kind of rose the tide up to getting it done? I mean that's pretty much the history of Apple. And right now it's kind of the same thing. You have these organizations, like working with Quantum and trying to be a Best Place to Work, or whatever the program is, they're trying to raise it up so that the measurement will help them improve.

Right. Bryan in a world where innovation is winning, I mean innovation flows from a very different kind of organization than efficiency does. It's not anti-efficiency; it doesn't mean that we're giving up on efficiency, because we need efficiency. But we've sort of gone to the extreme where efficiency is counter-productive. We've gotten to the point where we can't innovate because we're so caught in this trap I think. You're right Apple is a great example. Facebook is a great example of companies where your traditional managers would look at it and it's just going to look like chaos.

So does being data driven, digging into data, where does this really help companies initially Jason, like over the next six months? Because I really don't feel that as a profession that people don't look at it and go measurement and understanding more objectively what an organization is doing, is a bad thing. I just can't believe. I think if somebody is arguing to the counter of that, then they are so out of touch that I'm not sure they're long for being in the profession.

Right. They probably aren't listening to this Bryan.

Jason, so the next six months, where do you jump off and start making an impact and really get the most out? You know, trying to understand where data can really make a difference or drive more of an outcome that's positive for your organization.

Bryan, there are a couple of things in what we do around data. I think what we do around data is interesting because we're in the employee opinion, employee sentiment measurement space. So it's a little different, we're not counting tangible things and we're not tallying up tangible things. We're sort of making the invisible visible and sort of trying to capture the things that are more difficult to capture, or more difficult to understand. And a lot of times it something that we sort of sense or we feel.

I think there are a couple of things about being data driven, specifically around the kinds around the work that we're doing. We're really in the realm of let's call-it trying to measure and quantify culture and that kind of stuff. It's tough stuff because there's no way to independently go verify it. And so it would have to feel right.

But I think there are two things. I think the first key is I think making sure that you know what you're trying to measure and why. And I think throughout my career, throughout my interaction with HR, throughout my work in HR, one of the things that I think gets overlooked entirely too often is that we don't spend enough time with the intention of getting clear about why are we doing or what is it that we're trying to accomplish. And so even from a measurement perspective, engagement is an industry that I think is really interesting because the phrase "employee engagement" people throw around loosely as if everybody knows exactly what that is and that we're all talking about the same thing when we do that. And yet every single employee engagement vendor you talk to, or anybody that's in that business, they have a slightly different definition of engagement.

And so, as an organization, if you're going to measure employee engagement or if you're going to measure sentiment, or whatever it is, starting by getting clear about what exactly is it that you mean when you say that, and why it is important to you. Because definition is the first step of measurement and measurement is the first step in having data that you can use. It starts by being very clear and intentional about what you're measuring and why.

I feel then it's really then using the data to focus in on what matters. Just because you can measure it and just because it's off or the number isn't what you thought it would be doesn't mean you should take action on it. I think that's one of the big traps or issues we have with big data right now is that data has become omnipresent. It's everywhere. You can get data about anything and everything. And the problem is we almost have too much and I think some people think just because you have data means that it matters and means you should do something with it. Like in our engagement tool, one of the coolest things I think in the way we address engagement, and my favorite tool in there is we do sort of a statistical driver analysis. Which for us is just you measure a whole bunch of stuff and you collect a whole bunch of data and you're employees react to a whole lot of items, is that you can sort it by highest scoring and lowest scoring items. But the driver analysis tells you which items have the strongest statistical correlation to the overall engagement level of the employees.

For example, a lot of executive teams will get back their results and they'll see that that their benefit scores are low. And they'll start panicking because they're like man we put a whole bunch of money into this and why do people not like it? And so you look at and they're like do we need to put more money into this? What do we need to do? And it's like now wait a minute, let's back up for a second, because while that might be important to think about or talk about, the reality of it is its not driving engagement. So fixing your benefits isn't probably going to get you higher performance. If your benefits are really broken it might be a dissatisfier, you don't want to overlook it. But you want to get like what is really driving engagement? And in some organizations it's any range of things. But it's helping you zero in.

You only have so much effort; I mean time is the one commodity you have. Where should you put your time? I think that the reason that we measure and the reason we collect data is to focus our energies. If I was going to go all in on something, what should I go all in on that would have the biggest impact? And then let go of some of this other stuff. I think we're trying to do too much all the time. Trying to solve every problem. We don't need to solve every problem. Some problems are more important than others to solve. So I think that would be the two things from my experience that are really important.

Jason, we try to distill it down and in some cases where you can take action on it, like some of these topics are. The whole data conversation is a really big topic. And it's not a new topic, but we're now looking at it a different way. A lot more people are batting around and putting their toe in the water. The term "data" and now "big data" having a lot of ambiguity around those terms creates a heck of a lot of confusion. And I think people bail. When there's a lot of confusion people are risk adverse and they're like I don't want to get involved with that because I don't really understand it. A lot of times people don't convey that. But at the end of the day that's the underlying hesitance is the fact that if I don't understand it, I'm not going to get involved with it.

So what's the one thing that you've learned about being in the data the last twelve months, give or take? What's the one thing you're taking away like wow, I didn't really realize that until I was focused on this so much?

Bryan, I think it was just reinforcement for me of sort of the power of the scientific method if you will. Like have hypotheses but don't be so certain. Because there have been times where we did some research or we dug in where I thought something was true and it ended up being something different. When you're collecting data you really have to go into it being curious and open and be willing to understand that what you find might lead you in an entirely different direction than what you originally thought was true. And that's a good thing. So using data to challenge your base assumptions is really important. And using it to help you get smarter and do better work. At least that's been true for me. You have to have that open mind and be willing to ask questions.

Dr. Charles Handler, Rocket Hire

The "Caveman Principle"

Let's get to our guest, Dr. Charles Handler. Welcome to Thug Metrics.

Charles is the President and founder of Rocket Hire and full disclosure an Advisor to Assessment Research and Development, my mobile workforce assessment company.

For everyone, Rocket Hire is one of the longest standing organizations that focus in on screening and selection, in the global HR and assessment world. Helping people figure out all about what data is telling them and what data to use in the process.

So Charles, real briefly tell us a little bit about what you've got going on, and who you are. Then we'll jump into our conversation.

Sure, thanks Bryan. I have a Doctorate in Industrial Organizational Psychology, which can mean practitioners; training and viewpoint do a lot of different things. But I've specialized pretty much exclusively in helping organization to find and identify talent that is best suited for jobs. And those jobs are obviously things that produce revenue and bottom line impact for the company. So getting the right person in the right job is paramount. And we all know that when companies have great intentions in that area they often struggle in terms of being really able to execute something that can systematically deliver them the right talent. That's where we come in.

Charles, one of the questions we typically ask on the show is, for you, what's your definition of big data?

Right. Bryan that's a great question; I mean you can go with the classic, I think it's four or five "Vs." — volume, voracity, variety — off the top of my head I can't remember the other ones. When I've been asked to participate in big data related discussions, everybody kind of triangulates on that. But the reality of it is we're able to have the luxury now, and I don't use that word lightly, to work with even bigger and bigger datasets. Datasets that I would call three dimensional and I'm not a data scientist, so that may not be an official term that data scientists use, but it's the way I like to talk about conceptualizing a dataset. There are so many different variables and so many different interrelationships that it begins to become more of a matrix than it is just a couple of spreadsheets.

So for me, when I get an opportunity to work with a dataset that has a large amount of data like that, so that would be one aspect of it. Then the other one, for my definition is really that some of that data isn't data that you necessarily planted and harvested. It's not something that you exerted a lot of control over. It's something that you've been able to obtain and add into the mix of analysis. An example would be like scrapping Twitter feeds or something like that. So it's uncontrolled. I call it ballistic, which again is probably not a technical term. But it's just that it's out there doing its thing, and then we're going out there and grabbing it, pulling it into what we're looking at in our analysis and trying to make some sense out of it. To me when you start doing that, that's when the whole concept of working with big data kicks in.

Charles, I've heard probably one of the best definitions, discerning between big data and small, medium size data is if it can't be crunched and worked with to manipulate and analyze in Excel, then it is big data. Which I thought that was rather simple, but makes a lot of sense.

Right. Definitely Bryan.

You have to think about ultimately that strategy in your hiring, talent acquisition, and your daily life if you're a product person or a service person. For everybody, Charles is one of the leading mobile research people in the country, relative to screening and selection and the hiring process. So I think you're fairly dialed in to dig into this. Has mobile been more of a distraction? Is it a benefit? Tell us how it affects this whole data capture, like within your talent sector.

Bryan, I think it's just getting started with the assessment side of things. I think the job application side of things is obviously leading. And until companies get that piece figured out, the assessment piece of it is probably going to be riding a little bit closer to the caboose there. And that just tends to be how it has been with assessment implementation in general. You know, people getting their ATS in place first and everything. If you look at some of the studies – there are two kinds of studies out there that I think are very valuable – the first kind of study is more of an academic study. It's something I've had the opportunity to look at in pretty good detail. It shows there's really no difference fundamentally in how people respond and the quality of their responses, in terms of their liability and things like that, between a mobile device and another type of input, probably a desktop most likely.

In most areas, in cognitive areas I think there's still some debate or some scrutiny that's needed that's very justifiable. But beyond that part of data there's the research that looks at, it's less scientific more just kind of here's some numbers and things to think about. It's not still the case that most people are applying for jobs on mobile devices, nor are they taking assessments. So that may be because there's no availability, or because it's difficult. But it's obviously shifting into the public conscious. And I've had some good opportunity to work with mobile only and mobile first assessments. They work, and it's also a matter of aligning and structuring the assessment to be either really mobile or just a mobile rendering of HTML on a screen. And I think that's an important thing to consider. Overall though, we're in the infancy of this thing. We really are just getting started.

So there's really no line of sight Charles of really what a best practice is because there's really no standard? What I see, because everybody's trying to get it so it even works on a mobile assessment. Like in the early days, it's such a hodge-podge of where people are out on their strategy, if they have a strategy, what the strategy is. Nobody really knows on a broader scale.

Yes. I think that the way the conversation probably goes Bryan, is a talent leader says for this particular job, mobile application is going to be important. Maybe they partner with somebody who is already providing that opportunity and they say we want an assessment as well and we want that to be mobile. And if you went to the major vendors in the field right now, some of them would probably have a little bit of something for you. But there's not a lot. You could create your own. And in that case you'd be doing what I would suggest anybody who's interested in this do, which is understand what it is what you're trying to do first, and why it's valuable, early on in the process. Which is where I think mobile is probably going to find its most traction, as a screening tool, as an early tool for helping source and match.

Think about what things are important there and build them in a way you know will work and test them out the way that we know how to test stuff out. So there's not that huge of a deviation in the type of content. I think you obviously need to think about the delivery device. But that's another really interesting thing that happens when I talk to people about mobile and mobile assessment, is that we start talking about all the different things that define mobile. You can get a device with a screen of almost any size now, from every little gradation and sizing between a very small phone and a big tablet, even now a tablet that's also a laptop. There's less ability to define mobile as a five-inch screen. Some assessment experiences, and other type of experiences too, just as the screen size grows you're working your way into a better delivery medium and more opportunity to do stuff. That's interesting. The smaller the screen is, the more you really are forced into only one or two options for your item types. So there's still a lot of research there that needs to be done.

So the line of sight, in my mind Bryan, what's the business reason as to why we need this assessment to be mobile? And then what is it about this person we need to measure that we can boost up early in the process that's amenable to mobile? Then it's not necessarily that crazy, complex after that. There are plenty of people that can build apps that can do things. There are plenty of psychologists like myself that can measure something no matter how the input is coming in. The measurement side of things doesn't really change that much.

Charles, where do you feel there's a real void or blind spot, the intersection of using data and screening and selection in your workforce?

So using data and screening and selection in your workforce. Well, there isn't really one if you do it right because the data you collect in the hiring process has so much to tell you about your business. And it doesn't necessarily only tell you about how much your business is making or ROI. There's other information that is valuable that leads back to those ultimate answers. But it is really something that I think companies need to be aware of, but they need to first have a data-centric mindset. So to me it starts with thinking about having an internal data analytics team, even if it's one person. Having someone who owns and curates your data is going to be really important because that gives you the opportunity to start looking at different relationships tracking that could be of value to you. And in the screening process, not only where your talent is coming from, where you're best hires are coming from, where you're best hires aren't coming from.

And then, from a trait characteristics stand point, what is it that the most successful people and the longest tenure in this company have, and what are some things that people coming in the door need to have to be successfully here long term? That's important information as well. And that all comes from two streams, the stream of just the regular stuff you're collecting, and then some more Well that's a good question. I would say the first thing that popped into my mind is "garbage in garbage out." So the first thing is you've got to make sure the data you're collecting is aligned meaningfully to a bigger strategy. A lot of times what I find happening is most assessment vendors are more than happy to rerun validation studies or rerun kind of a directional, pointed studies that help look for relationships and things. And that's great. But really what you should be doing is kind of working toward a continual – and again it depends on the job too.

So one of the things I think is important that I haven't mentioned yet, is any time you're looking predictively with testing, the easy part is capturing the information about people through some kind of test or assessment or other bigger or broader screening data harvest. But when you look at that in a way that really can show you anything meaning, you have to have outcome variables, what we call the criteria variable, which is job performance. And that's where the whole thing kind of breaks down a lot of times for us when we're looking to do good things with data. I mean if you have a mid-level management, white-collar job it's very difficult to get hard line, bottom line ROI data about that person's performance. You can, depending if they supervise a unit or something, there's things you can look at, but it's not the same as an hourly lower level employee who may have a lot of obligation to show up on time. They may be providing a service to satisfy customers. They may be selling things and up-selling things. So all that stuff's track-able. Like a call center is a great example. Every single thing somebody does in a call center is track-able and is tracked. So we have a really great outcome data side too and then we can really become dangerous, because we can start looking at all kinds of different relationships between predictors and criteria. So when you have those two elements in place, a good data harvest on the front end and a good data tracking of performance on the other end, then you can build a system that continually looks at the lift.

We call it lift really, what's the advantage you get over hiring somebody with a certain predictive model that you've put in place. And that predictive model can be as simple as a big-five assessment tool. Or it could be as complicated as some real crazy algorithmic fractal machine that is just looking at all different kinds of equations. So there's a wide variety there. But at the end of the day ideally we want to know as fast as we can what the impact of predictive decisions are on valued outcomes. But we never check back in, which happens in a lot of situations with vendors who just aren't funded to do that work. Or it could be that we're continually checking in with what we call a "streaming validation system." It's kind of a system where data feeds are headed into a black box. I think about mobile being able to open that whole door up, because of two things.

First of all, people are bringing their own devices to work; we're allowing our workforce to have a good amount of window into that side of things. And on the other side of things, we're moving more and more towards your data and what you do on the job every day being tracked in your phone. And people are starting to become conditioned to that kind of data collection with fitness trackers, sleep trackers, eating trackers, and all that kind. So we're starting to track all kinds of stuff and as soon as the work related stuff gets moved into a phone or a wearable device, then we've got a whole new way to look at big data and try to find valuable relationships there. Anyway, that was probably a long-winded response, but I tied together I think a lot of important things to respond to that question.

Yeah Charles, it was a gigantic question, so great response. And you actually bring up two other incredibly interesting points that I think point to the future. First of all, let me give a brief amount of history. A long time ago, it used to be when you went from a paper and pencil selection tool, screening tool, everybody filled in the dots. When you went to a computer people were really concerned that there was going to be adverse impact. That people wouldn't be able to get to computers, different protected classes, just there were some economic barriers and lots of concerns around that. Those got ironed out and then it went to the web, and everybody had the same concern about validation and bias and screening tool. And then that went away. So now I'm curious, the research is indicating how mobile is affecting the bias and the screening and selection processes.

Right Bryan, that's a great question again. I think there are two answers to that that pop into my head. Answer number one is narrower. And that answer is that we really don't know yet the impact of cognitive tests that is math items, things like that, on mobile. We think maybe there's a distraction factor there that you have to be able to concentrate more. And there may be some other artifacts too, but it is not yet the case that we can correctly say there's no difference between cognitive tests on a mobile and non-mobile. That's where we're seeing differences. Outside of that there becomes a much broader and interesting thing to think about because we'll get that first one ironed out soon enough. That's just going to take a little bit more research and time and data.

But in the bigger picture we see that people are accessing everything they do more with a mobile device. In fact they don't have any other type of device in more of an urban setting, where the people have a different ethnic background than the cooler thing you think about in America, which is white male. So when you get into those urban environments, if you don't allow access through a mobile device, you're effectively cutting off part of your applicant population. When you look at the OFCCP and the EEOC look for, they may come at you about your testing, that's definitely something that can happen. But I've been there and I know for sure that they also look at the bigger picture of your organization. The diversity in your organization, the numbers, the applicants flow. All that stuff matters too. So you may have a test with no adverse impact on a non-mobile device, if you're not getting any opportunity for people in protected classes to take the test then you're effectively excluding them. So from diversity stand point, as much as you can do on mobile is ideal. I think that's something that you've got to think about really carefully.

Excellent. Next question Charles, and we're getting close to our last question here. Wearables. Wearable devises. Where is that going to play into maybe hiring or just workforce in general? I'm fascinated by this answer that you're going to bring me here.

Right, Bryan. Let's do it. Well, you know it's really interesting. So I'm going to expand the concept of wearables a little. I was just having a conversation with an I/O psychologist that works with a social technology company. I was talking with her about her thoughts on the future of things and where things are going. And she really brought up, without giving away any secrets or things like that – to qualify this I probably shouldn't have said the company that she works for – but at any rate, she talked a lot about the Oculus Rift acquisition by Facebook and how basically them and whoever else aren't going to start pushing even – we've seen the Google Glass thing already.

So when I think of wearables there are two things. There's the thing you instantly think of that's like a band or something that allows you to be tracked. Then there's something that you can wear on your face to augment reality, or something like that. And that's a wearable too, just a little bit different type of wearable. Maybe it can accomplish the same things and more, I don't know. There's a book I read, I believe it's called The Future of Work. There's more than one book called that, but it's one of by some MIT scientists who are convinced that by tracking everything everybody does in a workplace and collecting that data, they can help companies optimize all kinds of different things, from communication to infrastructure. And I think everybody I know universally who has read that book feels like it's creepy. And I think that everybody I know universally who's been asked to wear some kind of trackable device at work doesn't really like that very much.

So we're running into an issue that is not isolated to wearables, but is a bigger societal issue of how much computer and artificial intelligence and data collection and tracking are we comfortable with as people. It comes back to something that, again citing the book that I really like, a book called The Physics of the Future. In there and other books too he brings up this idea of what's called the "caveman principle" which is that humans want to touch and feel things, and have a very humanistic element in the collective. And when machines start coming and intruding too deeply into that people get very distrustful, and they don't really like it so much. So we'll see how people get acclimated to it when companies start asking them to do it. I think in some situations it makes more sense than others if you're working in a warehouse or doing something where what you're doing is really valuable to be tracked, if there can be efficiency that's one thing. If you're working at your mid-level management job and somebody is snooping in on everything that can be another thing.

That's excellent. It's kind of a different segment Charles, because I'm thinking people are hot or cold on this. To where if you started to look at a map to productivity based on whether somebody's hotter and colder, or how their body's reacting, like maybe they don't feel well or something like that, I think there's some interesting things that can happen. But I get that the creepy "big brother" perspective on that, by far.

Bryan, Yes. And I think though, what people don't know, if you're in a corporate mail system, something is probably scrapping all of your mail anyway. Sentiment analysis and some of these new technologies that are coming out are really going to change the game in terms of how we look at the things people are doing, and break those down into data bits that can be used to help evaluate and answer business problems, and optimize business.

So whether you have it on your wrist or you sign an agreement that you're corporate mail account is being scoured, those things are part and parcel of maybe the same thing.

www.ingramcontent.com/pod-product-compliance
Lightning Source LLC
Chambersburg PA
CBHW021929190326
41519CB00009B/958